THE PRIEST'S VADE MECUM

A MANUAL FOR THE VISITING
OF THE SICK

EDITED BY

T. W. CRAFER, D.D.

FOR
THE LITERATURE COMMITTEE
OF
THE GUILD OF S. RAPHAEL

LONDON
S·P·C·K
1961

COMMENDATION BY THE BISHOP OF ELY, WARDEN OF THE GUILD OF S. RAPHAEL

I am sure that there are many priests like myself who will find profit and instruction in this book. It is the fruit of many years' experience and is full of practical wisdom. I commend it to all who realize the need to make themselves more fitted to minister to the sick and suffering.

✠ Edward Ely

Ely,
 June 1945

First published 1945

FOREWORD

GENERATIONS of clergy have owed a debt of
gratitude to Bishop Walsham How for the help
given them in their parish work by his book *Pastor
in Parochia*. But its outlook is essentially that of
the nineteenth century, and clergy of to-day do
not care to use it. It is particularly in the prayers
and readings which it provides in the visiting of
the sick that it is felt to be out of touch with
present thought. There is therefore a real need
to provide something to take its place, and to
meet this need is the object of this book.
Many prayers have been taken over from the
former book, but only those that are consonant
with our present conception of the relation of
sickness to the will of God. Perhaps the significance of the change may best be realized by the
fact that *Pastor in Parochia* prefaced the section
dealing with the sick by the Office of the Visitation
of the Sick of the Prayer Book of 1662. *The
Priest's Vade Mecum* recommends instead the
Office contained in the 1928 Book, an Office
which was more drastically revised, both in
arrangement and in outlook, than any other.
It is only because leave cannot be given to repro-
duce it that it is not set in the forefront in this
book.

Pastor in Parochia contains much besides the Visitation of the Sick, but it must be left to others to revise the rest. What follows is a compilation from various sources, but its chief feature consists in the introductions to the various parts of ministry to the sick intended to give guidance to those who use the book, and particularly to the younger clergy.

The book is put forth by the Literature Committee of the Guild of St. Raphael, which has already produced two smaller books, one for the use of the sick, and the other for those who intercede for them.* This Guild represents the revival of the healing ministry of the Church on Anglican lines, and it is seeking to fulfil this ministry in strict accordance with what was laid down by the Lambeth Conference of 1930 in its report on Spiritual Healing. It is working under the patronage of the Archbishops of Canterbury and York, and some seventy other archbishops and bishops at home and overseas. It may therefore be said to be acting as the handmaid of the Church, and may claim to represent the changed thought of the Church to-day in its attitude towards sickness. Some of the introductions to sections have been contributed by priests of special experience who are not members of the Guild, and care has been taken not to press any par-

---

* *St. Raphael Prayer Book for the Use of the Sick*, and *St. Raphael Book of Prayers for the Sick for the Use of Intercession* (S.P.C.K.).

ticular or partisan views, but to provide a book which may be of real service to all in this difficult and responsible but truly joyful and Christlike part of a parish priest's ministry.

One of the Sub-Committees of the Lambeth Conference of 1930 dealt with the *Ministry of the Church*, which included a report on the Ministry of Healing. As a result, the whole Conference put forth the following resolutions:—

" Methods of Spiritual Healing, such as Unction or the Laying-on-of-Hands, should be used only in close conjunction with prayer and spiritual preparation.

" There is urgent need for close co-operation between clergy and doctors, since spiritual and physical treatment are complementary and equally necessary for true well-being.

" Seeing that the ministry of the Church is a ministry for the whole man, it is of the utmost importance that the clergy should equip themselves for a fuller understanding of the intimate connexion between moral and spiritual disorders and mental and physical ills " (p. 61).

The report quotes from " The Ministry of Healing ", which is itself the report of a committee appointed by the Lambeth Conference of 1920. In it the following words occur:—

" It is not the function of the Church to apply its means of restoration if no higher end is sought than the recovery of bodily health. Indeed, to do this would gravely compromise the meaning and purpose of the Church's rites and sacraments. No sick person must look to the clergyman to do what it is the physician's or surgeon's duty to do. . . . Whether the sick person throw off the sickness or not, the work of the Church will have been effective if he has thereby found truer peace of spirit and a more real knowledge of the uplifting presence and power of Christ."

Both Convocations have since issued a form for the administration of Holy Unction and the Laying-on-of-Hands. The Guild of St. Raphael publishes an address given to its members by Archbishop Lord Lang, when Primate, bearing the significant title of *Divine Healing, its Place in the Normal Ministry of the Church.*

CONTENTS

CONTENTS

INTRODUCTION

THE thought still lingers in the minds of many people that disease of body or mind is evidence of a divine visitation, that God is displeased with the sufferer and is seeking either to punish him or to correct him. In strange contrast to this may be found in the same minds a deep resentment should anyone suggest that the affliction is the result of sin. There is great confusion about the relationship between man and God where disease and suffering are concerned. The clergy are still too often regarded as heralds of death, and their office is thought of as being concerned only with the preparation of the soul for its passage into the next world. The offer of the Sacraments in times of sickness, and especially the suggestion that the sick person should receive Holy Communion, is taken to mean that the illness is very grave and likely to be fatal.

Few experienced priests would care to define the exact relation between sin and suffering, and although it is clear that in some cases the sufferer's sickness is plainly the direct outcome of his sinful life, it is equally clear that the saint is no more immune that the most unrepentant sinner. Nevertheless, it is more than difficult to attribute disease to the direct action of God who has created all things well and whose love sent forth his Son that while men were yet sinners they might be saved.*

The idea of a divine visitation in the form of disease dies hard, and it is no new thought, as we may learn from the question addressed to our Lord by his disciples concerning the man born blind, " Rabbi, who did sin, this man, or his parents, that he should be born blind? " (John 9. 2). Jesus the Incarnate God, who came to

---

* Reference may be made to G. E. Child's *A Parson's Thoughts on Pain* (pp. 5–7):

> " Evil is never God's will for any one; pain sometimes may be. It is clear both from Holy Scripture and our own experience that it is only too possible for men to thwart God's will and refuse to obey it. When that happens God has what we might call an ' alternative plan '. This does not mean a change in God. We must not think of him as continually altering his will for us in accordance with the turn of events, but all the while his primary will and the alternative plan are there; it is our own fault if the alternative plan becomes the only possible one. We must not ' blame ' God."

It is indeed true that God has allowed suffering to have a place in the education of the soul. Not all suffering is that caused by sickness, nor should it be confused with evil. The Church's answer to the problem created by the fact of suffering is not one which may be set forth with a major or minor premiss and brought to a satisfying logical conclusion. It is only by fortifying the soul in the hour of trial and by rendering the time of suffering profitable to spiritual advancement that God's purpose can be fulfilled and Christian souls saved from dismay and despair. Philosophical arguments are out of place in the sick-room; prayer and the sacraments are the means by which God's love and grace are brought near to transmute what may seem to be purposeless suffering into spiritual blessing. But this is entirely different from the all too widespread thought of suffering as a divine visitation of displeasure.

2

reveal to mankind the true character of the Father, did not give the answer to this age-long question by entering upon a lengthy verbal explanation. It was given in action. The hand stretched out to heal was never the hand put forth to strike with plague. "Jesus went about all the cities and villages, teaching in their synagogues, and preaching the Gospel of the Kingdom, and healing all manner of disease and all manner of sickness" (Matt. 9. 35). It is not only in connexion with preaching, but in regard to healing that Jesus bade his disciples declare to men, "The Kingdom of God is nigh unto you". Thus by his healing works did the Lord of Life make known the will of his Father to heal and to save all who would draw nigh unto him in faith and repentance.

Nor did Jesus confine this ministry to himself, either in his own lifetime or afterwards, for he bade his disciples go before him into every city and place whither he himself was about to come, charging them to "heal the sick that are therein, and say unto them, The Kingdom of God is come nigh unto you" (Luke 10. 9). With a similar commission he sent forth the twelve (Matt. 10. 2 and Luke 9. 1f.). To this he added his promise recorded in Mark 16. 17f.

The Church's ministry to the sick in fulfilment of this commission, and the realization of the promise made by Christ, do not end with the healing works recorded in the book of the Acts of the Apostles. There has never been a complete cessation of such works of healing, although it must be admitted that in later ages it is often difficult to separate the true from the spurious. Furthermore, throughout the centuries the Church has sought, by the founding of hospitals and nursing orders and by its contributions to the science of medicine, to perpetuate the preaching of the Gospel by its work for the sick. It cannot do otherwise without failing to present the Gospel in its entirety and to accept the responsibility which its Head has laid upon it.

In later days the care of the sick has appeared to become the concern of a special body of highly trained people, and it has consequently been assumed that it is no longer any business of the Church as such. But we make a great mistake if we are content to think that the work of healing has passed wholly into the hands of those who work mainly by material agencies. Nobody with experience of spiritual work among the sick can fail to realize how real and necessary a part in the work of healing falls to the priest in his pastoral care.

Perhaps the chief significance of the change which has taken place in the ministry to the sick in recent years is that no longer may we confine our pastoral solicitude for the sufferer to consolatory counsels, nor even to absolution in preparation for death; but we are returning to the apostolic and primitive conception of that ministry as being charged with the definite work of restoration to health.

Healing, in the fullest sense of the term, must be the restoration to harmonious working of the whole being. A cure of the physical disability is not a healing if the mental or spiritual maladjustment of the sick man's life leaves the door open to further ills, as often it may do. Jesus applied his healing power to all three parts of man's personality, for he healed the physically afflicted, the lunatic and those whose distress was due to spiritual disorder or to sin. There is no part of the human being which is beyond the reach of God's healing power. Therefore religious ministrations must always be directed towards the healing of the whole man, and have for their main object that the sufferer may be brought into the closest communion with the Lord and Giver of life.

Some forms of faith-healing will always be repugnant to both doctors and clergy alike, nor would they find support in the practice of the apostolic age or of the primitive Church. Yet none would deny the importance and efficacy of faith as taught by Jesus. Moreover, none know better than the doctors themselves the limitations of purely material remedies. But in the sacramental system of the Church we have that meeting of the material and spiritual values which alone can satisfy the needs of men in health and sickness. Because man is both a material and a spiritual being, the use of the one to the exclusion of the other will always fall short of the best.

The sacraments of Holy Communion, Holy Unction, and Absolution touch our lives at their spiritual centre, and by them every legitimate material remedy can be reinforced. These are independent of the worthiness of the minister and of any special healing gift with which he may have been endowed or which he may lack. Certainly the personality of the minister may count for much, but the Sacraments do not depend on it. Every priest faithfully ministering the Sacraments brings to the sick the utmost which God has to give.

The Laying-on-of-Hands stands on a different level from the Sacraments, though it may be spoken of as sacramental. A generation ago, at the beginning of the revival of the Church's ministry of healing, it was only certain individuals, lay as well as clerical, who offered to Christ and his Church some special healing power which they were already felt to possess. Parish priests seldom claimed to use this form of ministration by virtue of their priesthood; but, if they were in favour of such a ministry, they were content to call in an " expert " to some particular case of sickness. But this outlook is now changed. It is felt that, if the priest makes use of Holy Unction, the lesser thing is included in the greater, and he may also use the Laying-on-of-Hands by virtue of his priesthood. Moreover, throughout his ministry he is acting in the name of the whole Church, for it is in the Church as the Body of Christ that the power resides, and the priest is acting as the Church's representative.

All this is something more than theory, and is supported by the actual experience of priests without number. No priest need be afraid to give the Laying-on-of-Hands, provided that he has helped the sufferer to make due and careful preparation for it, and to recognize that it is no mere bodily cure that is being sought, but the strengthening of his whole personality for the service of God. God's blessing so manifestly rests on such a ministry that, even in cases where obstacles to bodily healing remain, there is a spiritual uplift that brings new peace of mind.*

The laity, as well as the clergy, have a real part in that ministry by their work of intercession. Indeed, one could wish that in every parish there might be found a small band of intercessors who would be in church to pray while the priest goes forth to visit. The laity have still much to learn about their share in the ministry to the sick and the enkindling of that corporate faith in the midst of which many mighty works may be wrought.

Although it is true that a large proportion of doctors have little understanding of the Church's faith and sacraments, increasing numbers are aware of the value which is to be attached to

---

* See R. R. Spread, *Stretching Forth Thy Hands to Heal*, Ch. VIII, on " The Parish Priest and Spiritual Healing ".

careful and intelligent ministrations. There is a great readiness to co-operate with the clergy when it is perceived that through them the patient finds the mental and spiritual help which reinforces all other aid given to him. Many doctors are very willing to confer with the priest, and some will plainly state their recognition of the primary importance of spiritual ministrations in specific cases. It is much to be desired that the spiritual care of the sick shall be so carried out that such co-operation may be more and more sought.

This little book has been compiled in the hope that it may help to supply some guidance and material that will make the ministry to the sick not only easier to perform, but such as is consonant with Our Lord's commission and commendable to those members of the medical profession who know the value of such a ministry.

SERVICES AND DEVOTIONS WITH THE SICK

I. THE FIVE OFFICES OF THE PRAYER BOOK AS PROPOSED IN 1928

THESE five brief offices, each with a different purpose, replace the one long and clumsy Office of 1662, and their attitude towards sickness shows a return to that of the early Church. The priest may regard them as stages in the work of visitation, implying an objective throughout.

The First Office is of a general kind, and can, when desired, be used as an introduction to those less formal prayers which most priests will like to use in their own words, adapted to the special needs of each case. The change of attitude may be seen in the prayer, " May it be thy good pleasure to restore him to his former health, that so he may live the rest of his life in thy fear and to thy glory ".

The Second Office is entitled *Exhortation to Faith and Prayer*. The exhortation simply indicates the lines which the priest may follow in his own informal talk leading to the rehearsing of the Articles of the Faith. Scope is given for helping the sick man to seek wholeness in the Name and power of Jesus, in the words " Our Lord, manifested in the Gospel as the healer of disease, is still ready to minister grace for the healing of the body ". And, on the other hand, help is given

B

9

for the facing of pain in the words " There is great honour in suffering if by our pain we are conformed to the Spirit of Jesus Christ; for in the bearing of pain God manifested his will to redeem the world ".

The rubric which follows, bidding the priest to explain " some part of the Christian Faith ", suggests two things:—

> (i) He may choose some particular belief in which he has found the sick person to be lacking.
> (ii) He may, especially in the case of long sickness, link his exhortation with any festival which the Church may then be keeping.

Before the actual saying of the Creed, it is helpful to remind the sick person that it is " the profession of faith which you made unto God in your Baptism "; for in many cases the fact may long have been forgotten. He should be told that his response "All this I steadfastly believe " was said then in his name by his god-parents. In these days there are many who have not been baptized, and this mention of Baptism may help the priest to make sure about this.

The final rubric extends the exhortation from faith to prayer, to help the sick person " so to order his rule of prayer, for himself and others, that his day of sickness may be a time of faithful and loving intercourse with God ". This gives the opportunity of suggesting to him a " rule of prayer ", but, except in cases of long invalidism, it must be a very easy one.

The Third Office is entitled *Exhortation to Repentance.* The opening rubrics are the same as the first and fourth of those in the 1662 Book, and a difficult task is involved in the first words, " The minister shall examine the sick person ".

He will need to be in spiritual touch with him before he can attempt to do this, and this is suggested by this being the third in a series of offices. Part of the examination is on the same lines as those of the answer to the last question in the Catechism, " What is required of them who come to the Lord's supper? " In cases where this is likely to be familiar, it might form a useful basis for the " examination ".

This office is far more than an " exhortation " to repentance, for it makes provision for a sacramental act of confession and absolution. In many cases this can only be after the priest has given much help of an informal kind, such as is outlined later in this book, on page 67, under the heading *Outline of Talks on Repentance and Confession.*

The opening words of Confession are given in their simplest form, and, where necessary, the penitent should be told them, or given a copy of them beforehand, and in some cases helped in the saying of them, as follows:—

" I confess to God Almighty, the Father, the Son, and the Holy Ghost, that I have sinned in thought, and word, and deed, through my own most grievous fault; wherefore I pray God to have mercy on me. And especially I have sinned in these ways . . ."

The Office does not add the final words, to be said after the particular sins have been specified, but the penitent to whom this Sacrament is not familiar should be taught to conclude with words like these :—

" For these and all my other sins which I cannot now remember, I am heartily sorry, I humbly ask pardon of God, and steadfastly purpose amendment of life; and of you, my father, I ask for penance, counsel and advice, and that you will pray for me to the Lord our God."

The form of Absolution is, of course, the regular form, for use with the whole as well as the sick, already given in the 1662 Book.

For this sacramental office, which should not be used at the same time as the informal " examination " which precedes it, the priest will bring surplice and stole, unless prevented by emergency.

The Fourth Office is entitled *An Act of Prayer and Blessing*. This is a substitute for the use of Psalm 71 and the prayer which follows it in the 1662 Book.

The Antiphon " O Saviour of the world " is rightly placed at the beginning of the psalm as well as at the end, and is one that may be frequently used at the beginning of ministrations to the sick.

The substitution of Psalm 121, " I will lift up mine eyes unto the hills ", for the gloomy Psalm 71 illustrates our changed attitude towards sickness.

Useful suggestions for alternative psalms include 23, 27, 43, 77, 86, 91, 103, 142, 146. Only the first seventeen verses of Psalm 71 are suggested if that psalm is used. But the concluding verses will be found appropriate for use when recovery from sickness has begun.

The prayer which follows is one for healing.

" O Almighty God, who art the giver of all health and the aid of them that seek to thee for succour: We call upon thee for thy help and goodness mercifully to be shewed upon thy servant, that being healed of his infirmities, he may give thanks unto thee in thy Holy Church; through Jesus Christ our Lord. *Amen.*"

A definite step forward in the revival of the Church's Ministry of Healing is made by the suggestion that the priest shall say the prayer " laying his hand upon the sick person if desired ".

This makes for recognition of a revived Ministry of Healing as part of the province and responsibility of the Church towards the sick. No more seems to be suggested than an informal act, not necessarily preceded by preparation. But whenever it is possible, the sick person should be prepared by definite acts of repentance and faith, and a fuller and more formal use made of an office for the Laying-on-of-Hands. Such an Office was published and sanctioned by both Convocations in 1935.

In the book sanctioned by the Convocations there is a form for the Administration of Holy Unction. The two Offices for Laying-on-of-Hands and Holy Unction will be found on pages 30 and 32 of this book.

The Fifth Office contains *Special Prayers to be used as Occasions may Serve.*

The Litany for the Sick and Dying has the advantage of brevity, but if a longer form is desired it will be found among " Prayers for the Dying " on page 111 of this book, where a Commendation will also be found.

Among the other prayers, the first place is given to a prayer for healing, and the prayer *for a Convalescent* is a useful addition.

The Five Offices conclude with a *Note* suggesting prayers and passages of Holy Scripture for use with the sick, the prayers consisting of twenty-five Collects from the Prayer Book, while the passages of Scripture are given under twenty headings, beginning with *Confidence in God* and ending with *Christian Hope on the approach of Death.*

A longer list of suitable passages is given on page 56 of this book.

II. THE COMMUNION OF THE SICK

(a) *General Considerations*

IN visiting the sick the priest will at once find out whether the sick person has been confirmed. If so, he will turn his thoughts to the receiving of what is in the fullest sense the Sacrament of Life.

Whether he be a regular or an occasional communicant, or have long ceased to be a communicant at all, he will need to be gently drawn towards the desire for this Sacrament.

Even with a regular communicant laid aside by illness, there is often a hesitation, and he says he would rather wait till he is better and able to receive in church. It should be pointed out to him that now is the time he needs it, for it is the sacrament of wholeness, in body and mind as well as spirit. This point may be summed up in some words of Archbishop Lang :—

> " In the Sacrament of our Lord's Body and Blood is achieved that most full and real union of the human spirit with the Spirit of Christ, out of which all blessing, mental, spiritual and physical, must necessarily flow. Sometimes too little notice is taken of the fact that the words of administration refer to the body as well as the soul, and that the Holy Communion is given for preserving of life, both bodily and spiritually. You cannot possibly make any mistake when you em-

phasize the importance, not only for the spiritual life, but for the physical and mental life, of that most wonderful Sacrament."

The occasional communicant may hesitate for a different reason, fearing that the Sacrament is meant as a preparation for death. Often those of his household may discourage it on the ground that it will depress the sick man. It will be a help to give them the words of the Archbishop on the subject.

With the lapsed communicant his illness provides a great opportunity to bring him back to the claiming of the privilege which he has neglected. He will need to be helped towards acts of repentance and faith, and made to feel that our Lord means him to use his sickness for this fresh act of union with him.

In cases of chronic sickness the priest will of course communicate his sick folk regularly, giving them the service of the Church's seasons and helping them to realize their fellowship with the rest of the Church. Any hesitation on their part at not having a fresh consecration may be overcome by showing them that the reserved Sacrament is a link with the worship of the Church.

In some cases where the sick person has not been confirmed, the chance of preparing him may be opened up. In grave illness, where some preparation is possible, the rubric " ready and willing to be confirmed " may be made use of, after receiving the permission of the bishop to communicate him.

(b) *Forms of Service*

(i) *FOR THE CELEBRATION OF THE HOLY COMMUNION IN THE HOUSE OF THE SICK*

The Prayer Book Service is published in booklet form by S.P.C.K. as *The Communion of the Sick.*

The Administration of the Blessed Sacrament in Private Houses is a booklet (S.P.C.K.) containing " a few practical instructions and simple devotions which could be put into the hands of sick people of but little education ". These include forms of preparation and thanksgiving.

The following Collect, Epistle and Gospel may be substituted (from the Priest's Prayer Book).

The Collect.

O GOD, who alone canst strengthen the weakness of man : Show forth thy mighty help unto this thy sick servant, that by thy merciful aid *he* may be restored whole to thy Church; through Jesus Christ our Lord. *Amen.*

The Epistle. 1 John 3. 21, 22

BELOVED, if our heart condemn us not, then have we confidence towards God. And whatsoever we ask, we receive of Him, because we keep His commandments, and do those things that are pleasing in His sight.

The Gospel. John 6. 56–58

JESUS said, He that eateth my flesh, and drinketh my blood, dwelleth in me, and I in him. As the living Father hath sent me, and I live by the Father: so he that eateth me, even he shall live by me. This is that bread which came down from heaven: not as your fathers did eat manna, and are dead: he that eateth of this bread shall live for ever.

Prayer after Communion.

O LORD, Holy Father, Almighty, Everlasting God, we humbly beseech thee that the Holy Communion of the Body and Blood of thy Son Jesus Christ our Lord may be for salvation of soul and body to this our *brother* who hath received it; through the same Jesus Christ our Lord. *Amen.*

(ii) *FOR ADMINISTERING THE HOLY COMMUNION BY MEANS OF THE RESERVED SACRAMENT*

The priest will use at least the Collect of the day, the Confession and Absolution, the Prayer of Humble Access; and, after Communion, the Lord's Prayer and the Blessing. But in cases of lesser or chronic sickness, the sick man will often be glad of more of the Service, such as the Sursum Corda, etc., the Prayer of Thanksgiving, and the *Gloria in excelsis.*

(iii) *FOR SPIRITUAL COMMUNION*

A Service of Corporate Spiritual Communion is published by S.P.C.K. and S.P.G.

An Act of Spiritual Communion

St. Raphael Prayer Book for the use of the Sick, Part VII, pp. 40–43.

III. OFFICES FOR HOLY UNCTION AND THE LAYING-ON-OF-HANDS

(a) *Holy Unction*

It may be well to begin by quoting the words of Archbishop Lord Lang:

" The Convocation of Canterbury has authorized and published forms of service for the use of Unction which are in accordance with ancient precedent and true principles; therefore it may be considered that within the normal exercise of the ministry of the priesthood there is the exercise of the ministry of Unction and the Laying-on-of-Hands. . . . In its true sense the ministry of Unction is not focused directly upon the curing of the body, but, first and foremost, upon the settling, quieting and strengthening of the spirit by the increase of faith in God, trust in him, and submission to his Will. . . . That is why you are right always in attaching such importance to the preparation of the individual to whom this ministry is given."

If the parish priest has any hesitation in making use of this lesser sacrament of the Church, the following points are suggested:—

1. When our Lord first called his disciples to use the healing ministry in his Name, they "anointed with oil many that were sick, and healed them" (Mark 6. 13).

2. The custom of the primitive Church is seen in the charge given in James 5. 14–16: "Let him call for the elders of the Church: and let them pray over him, anointing him with oil in the name of the Lord, etc."

3. The reference in this passage to the confession and forgiveness of sins suggests, and has always suggested, that a sacramental confession and absolution should precede the anointing with oil.

4. It was not until the Middle Ages, and then only in the Western Church, that the sacrament of healing became a sacrament of death, and all the stress came to be laid on its effect on the soul, and not on the body. The Eastern Church has never ceased to use Holy Oil in ministering to the sick.

5. At the Reformation the original use was restored in the First Prayer Book of Edward VI, and, though subsequently omitted, the form and actual words have now received the authority of both Convocations.

6. The recently revised and extended use of Holy Unction has been attended by plainly manifested blessings. It is no longer felt that it is only meant for those in danger of death, or that it can only be administered once in any one illness.

The sick person must be carefully prepared beforehand, and made to understand that, whether the healing extends to his body or not, it begins in his soul, which must first be cleansed and prepared. In grave illness this may have to be done hastily. In other cases it may be useful to give him something to read for himself, such as *A Little Book about Unction*, by Purcell Fox ; or a pamphlet, *Helps in Preparing for Holy Unction*, which may be had from the Secretary of the Guild of St. Raphael.

Most diocesan bishops are now ready to bless oil for priests who require it, and in some dioceses Holy Oil is always ready for their use. Application may also be made to the Guild of St. Raphael, as above.

The priest should see that similar preparations are made to those for a private Communion. It is well to have a plate or paten on which to place the stock containing the Holy Oil, and cotton-wool will be needed (instead of water), with which to wipe the sick person's forehead after anointing and also the thumb of the priest himself.

THE ORDER FOR THE ANOINTING OF THE SICK

The priest, wearing a surplice and stole, shall bring the glass or silver stock containing the hallowed oil, and, placing it on the table, shall say the following psalm, with this Antiphon before and after.

If on account of weakness it is necessary to shorten the service, the priest may omit the Psalm and the prayers marked with a *.

Antiphon: O Saviour of the world, who by thy Cross and precious Blood hast redeemed us: Save us and help us, we humbly beseech thee, O Lord.

Psalm 23

THE Lord is my shepherd: therefore can I lack nothing.

He shall feed me in a green pasture: and lead me forth beside the waters of comfort.

He shall convert my soul: and bring me forth in the paths of righteousness, for his Name's sake.

Yea, though I walk through the valley of the shadow of death, I will fear no evil: for thou art with me; thy rod and thy staff comfort me.

Thou shalt prepare a table before me against them that trouble me: thou hast anointed my head with oil, and my cup shall be full.

But thy loving-kindness and mercy shall follow me all the days of my life: and I will dwell in the house of the Lord for ever.

Glory be to the Father, and to the Son: and to the Holy Ghost;

As it was in the beginning, is now, and ever shall be: world without end. *Amen.*

Antiphon: O Saviour of the World, who by thy Cross and precious Blood hast redeemed us: Save us and help us, we humbly beseech thee, O Lord.

Or Psalm 31

Or Psalm 71 *may be said*

A Short Lesson

James 5. 14, 15

Is any among you sick? let him call for the elders of the church; and let them pray over him, anointing him with oil in the name of the Lord: and the prayer of faith shall save him that is sick, and the Lord shall raise him up, and if he have committed sins, it shall be forgiven him.

If the sick person hath not already made confession of sins and received absolution, then shall be said this form of confession.

I CONFESS to God Almighty, the Father, the Son, and the Holy Ghost, in the sight of the whole company of heaven, that I have sinned exceedingly in thought, word, and deed, through my fault, my own fault, my own most grievous fault. Wherefore I pray God Almighty, the Father, the Son, and the Holy Ghost, to have mercy upon me.

23

Then shall the priest say,

MAY the Almighty and merciful Lord grant you pardon, absolution, and remission of all your sins, space for true repentance, amendment of life, and the grace and comfort of His Holy Spirit. *Amen.*

Then shall the priest say,

The Lord be with you.
Answer: And with thy spirit.
Priest: Let us pray.
Lord, have mercy upon us.
Christ, have mercy upon us.
Lord, have mercy upon us.

OUR Father, which art in heaven, Hallowed be thy Name. Thy kingdom come. Thy will be done, in earth as it is in heaven. Give us this day our daily bread. And forgive us our trespasses, As we forgive them that trespass against us. And lead us not into temptation; But deliver us from evil. *Amen.*

℣. O Lord, save thy servant;
℟. Who putteth *his* trust in thee.
℣. Send *him* help from thy holy place:
℟. And evermore mightily defend *him.*
℣. Help us, O God of our salvation;
℟. And for the glory of thy Name deliver us, and be merciful to us sinners, for thy Name's Sake.

[*If the oil is to be then hallowed, the priest, standing, shall say the following prayer,*

24

O ALMIGHTY Lord God, who hast taught us by thy holy Apostle St. James to anoint the sick with oil, that they may recover their health and render thanks unto thee for the same: Ble✠ss this oil, we beseech thee, that whosoever may be anointed therewith, may be delivered from all troubles of body and mind, and from every assault of the powers of evil; through Jesus Christ our Lord. *Amen.*]

Here the priest shall lay both his hands upon the sick person's forehead, saying as follows :

O ALMIGHTY God, who art the giver of all health, and the aid of them that seek to thee for succour: We call upon thee for thy help and goodness mercifully to be showed upon this thy servant, that being healed of *his* infirmities, *he* may give thanks unto thee in thy holy church; through Jesus Christ our Lord. *Amen.*

Then the priest, dipping his thumb in the holy oil, shall anoint the sick person on the forehead, in the form of a Cross, saying,

N. I anoint thee with holy oil In the Name of the Father, and of the Son, and of the Holy Ghost. *Amen.*

As with this visible oil thy body outwardly is anointed: So our heavenly Father, Almighty God, grant thee of his infinite goodness that thy soul inwardly may be anointed with the Holy Ghost, who is the Spirit of all strength, comfort, relief, and gladness: and vouchsafe for his great mercy (if it be his blessed will) to restore unto thee thy bodily health and strength, to serve him; and send thee release of all thy pains, troubles, and diseases, both in body and mind; through Jesus Christ our Lord, who by his death hath overcome death, and with the Father and the Holy Ghost evermore liveth and reigneth, God, world without end. *Amen.*

After the anointing the priest shall, with the wool, remove the oil from the forehead of the sick person, and from his own hand. The wool is to be burned after the Service.

Then the priest shall say,

Let us give thanks to God for the gift which he has bestowed upon this his servant.

Silence will be kept for a space.

Then the priest shall say,

The Lord be with you.
Answer : And with thy spirit.

Priest : Let us pray.

OUR Father, which art in heaven, Hallowed be thy Name. Thy kingdom come. Thy will be done, in earth as it is in heaven. Give us this day our daily bread. And forgive us our trespasses, As we forgive them that trespass against us. And lead us not into temptation; But deliver us from evil: For thine is the kingdom, the power and the glory, For ever and ever. *Amen.*

*O CHRIST our Lord, Redeemer of the souls and bodies of men: Be pleased, we pray thee, to perfect the work of thy healing grace in this thy servant; that *his* bodily strength being renewed, if so it seem good unto thee, *he* may be strengthened with might ever more and more in the inner man, and may be fitted at last for that life wherein there shall be no more sickness nor pain; for thy Name and mercy's sake grant this, O Lord, who, with the Father and the Holy Spirit, livest and reignest, God over all, blessed for evermore. *Amen.*

Then the priest shall say,

*THE Almighty Lord, who is a most strong tower to all them that put their trust in him, to whom all things in heaven, in earth, and under the earth do bow and obey, be now and evermore thy defence; and make thee know and feel, that there is none other name under heaven given to man, in whom, and through whom, thou mayest receive health and salvation, but only the Name of our Lord Jesus Christ. *Amen.*

UNTO God's gracious mercy and protection we commit thee. The Lord bless thee, and keep thee. The Lord make his face to shine upon thee, and be gracious unto thee. The Lord lift up his countenance upon thee, and give thee peace, both now and evermore. *Amen.*

℣. The Lord be with you.
℟. And with thy spirit.

27

THANKS be to God who giveth us the victory through our Lord Jesus Christ.

℣. Let us depart in peace.

℟. In the Name of Christ. *Amen.*

(b) *The Laying-on-of-Hands*

This rite may be used more freely than Holy Unction. In some cases it may be used as leading up to it, or in conjunction with it, immediately before the anointing. Also after an anointing, if the sick person desires such ministry before the time seems to have come for another anointing, the Laying-on-of-Hands should be given.

The form following is meant for a formal act of ministry, to be carefully prepared for by acts of repentance and faith, and used as an Office, either whole or in shortened form where necessary. But it is recognized that the priest may also lay his hands on the sick in blessing in less formal ways.

In this case no formal service will be used, and the priest, after brief prayer with the sick person and a few words explaining what he is about to do, will lay hands upon him with some such words as these:—

> "The grace of the Lord Jesus flow forth upon thee for the healing of soul and mind and body, upon whom we now lay hands in his most holy Name."

If a priest, though ready to use Holy Unction by virtue of his priesthood, has any hesitation in doing himself what, in the revival of the healing ministry, has often been left to those who, by virtue of a gift of healing, have been regarded as specialists in this ministry, the following points are suggested to him.

1. He is acting, as in the Sacramental Ministry of Unction, as a priest possessed of the grace of Holy Orders, with a power and an authority which is not personal but resides in the Church which he represents.

2. If he may use Holy Unction, he may also use the Laying-on-of-Hands, for the less is contained in the greater.

3. The use of the Laying-on-of-Hands is provided for in the Prayer Book of 1928 set forth by the episcopate.

4. If outside help is sought, except in cases where it is especially asked for, the priest's own ministry to those for whom he is responsible is somewhat lessened, and it becomes less easy for him to have the understanding and co-operation of the doctor whose patient is ministered to.

With regard to the actual technique of this ministry, it is well to see that the sick person assumes a relaxed and comfortable position, though there are many cases where the attitude of kneeling is possible. This is specially true when it is possible to give the ministry in church, in the presence of those who may help by their prayers. A chair (if necessary) may be placed in front of the altar rails, and a kneeling position taken when the actual ministry is given, the priest standing within the rails.

Both hands should be laid firmly on the sick person's head all the while that the words are being said, " In the Name of God Most High ", etc.

Where the service is formal and specially prepared for, some help in preparing should be given, such as the pamphlets of the Guild of St. Raphael: *Some Thoughts for the Preparing for Divine Healing*, and *For Those who Wish to Hear about Divine Healing*.

FORM FOR THE LAYING-ON-OF-HANDS

One of the Psalms following shall be said, at the Minister's discretion, with this Anthem before and after :

Antiphon : O Saviour of the world, who by thy Cross and precious Blood has redeemed us : save us and help us, we humbly beseech Thee, O Lord.

Psalm 91

WHOSO dwelleth under the defence of the most High : shall abide under the shadow of the Almighty.

I will say unto the Lord, Thou art my hope, and my strong hold : my God, in him will I trust.

For he shall deliver thee from the snare of the hunter : and from the noisome pestilence.

He shall defend thee under his wings, and thou shalt be safe under his feathers : his faithfulness and truth shall be thy shield and buckler.

Thou shalt not be afraid for any terror by night : nor for the arrow that flieth by day.

There shall no evil happen unto thee : neither shall any plague come nigh thy dwelling.

For he shall give his angels charge over thee : to keep thee in all thy ways.

They shall bear thee in their hands : that thou hurt not thy foot against a stone.

Thou shalt go upon the lion and adder : the young lion and the dragon shalt thou tread under thy feet.

Glory be to the Father, and to the Son : and to the Holy Ghost; *As it was in the beginning, is now, and ever shall be : world without end. Amen.*

Or,

Psalm 71

If the Confession and Absolution of the Sick is not used here, then shall one of the General Confessions and Absolutions be said at the discretion of the Minister. Or the form of Confession and Absolution may be used as given in the Order for the Anointing of the Sick, *page 23.*

Minister : Let us pray.

SILENT PRAYER

Lord, have mercy upon us.
Christ, have mercy upon us.
Lord, have mercy upon us.

Our Father, which art in heaven, Hallowed be thy Name; Thy kingdom come; Thy will be done; In earth as it is in heaven. Give us this day our daily bread. And forgive us our trespasses, As we forgive them that trespass against us. And lead us not into temptation; but deliver us from evil. *Amen.*

℣. O Lord, save thy servant;

℞. Who putteth *his* trust in thee.

℣. Send *him* help from thy holy place;

℞. And evermore mightily defend *him.*

℣. Help us, O God of our salvation;

℞. And for the glory of thy Name deliver us, and be merciful to us sinners, for thy Name's sake.

℣. O Lord, hear our prayer;

℞. And let our cry come unto Thee.

Let us pray.

O Almighty God, who art the giver of all health, and the aid of them that seek to thee for succour: We call upon thee for thy help and goodness mercifully to be shewed upon this thy servant, that being healed of *his* infirmities, *he* may give thanks unto thee in thy holy Church; through Jesus Christ our Lord. *Amen.*

Silent Prayer

Then the Minister, standing by the sick person, shall lay both his hands upon the head of the same, saying the words :

In the Name of God most High, may release from thy pain be given thee, and thy health be

32

restored according to his holy will. In the Name of Jesus Christ, the Prince of Life, may new life quicken thy mortal body. In the Name of the Holy Spirit, mayest thou receive inward health, and the peace which passeth all understanding.

And the God of all peace himself sanctify you wholly; and may your spirit and soul and body be preserved entire, without blame at the coming of our Lord Jesus Christ. *Amen.*

Let us pray.

SILENT PRAYER

℣. The voice of joy and health is in the dwellings of the righteous:

℟. The right hand of the Lord bringeth mighty things to pass.

O ALMIGHTY Lord, and everlasting God, vouchsafe, we beseech thee, to direct, sanctify, and govern, both our hearts and bodies, in the ways of thy laws, and in the works of thy commandments; that through thy most mighty protection, both here and ever, we may be preserved in body and soul; through our Lord and Saviour Jesus Christ. *Amen.*

UNTO God's gracious mercy and protection we commit thee. The Lord bless thee, and keep thee. The Lord make his face to shine upon thee, and be gracious unto thee. The Lord lift up His countenance upon thee, and give thee peace, both now and evermore. *Amen.*

IV. PRAYERS FOR USE WITH THE SICK

1. *For Healing*

O LORD Jesus Christ, who by the power of thy word didst heal all who were brought unto thee in the days of thy flesh: Mercifully help thy servant in *his* hour of need: grant, if it be thy will, that by the same power *he* may be delivered from sickness and restored to health, and may for ever hereafter serve thee in newness of life to the glory of thy Name; who livest and reignest with the Father and the Holy Ghost, ever one God, world without end. *Amen.*

O ALMIGHTY Father, who dost heal both the bodies and the souls of men, who didst send thine only-begotten Son, our Lord Jesus Christ, to heal every sickness and disease, and to redeem us from death: Deliver this thy servant, we humbly beseech thee, from all infirmities, both of body and soul, which do hinder *him*, and quicken *him* by the grace of thy Christ; for thou art the fountain of healing, O our God; and unto thee do we give the glory with thine only-begotten Son; who with thee and the Holy Ghost liveth and reigneth ever one God, world without end. *Amen.*

O HOLY Lord, Almighty Father, Everlasting God, who dost confirm the frailty of our nature by pouring upon it thine exceeding goodness, that our limbs and bodies may be strengthened by the healthful medicine of thy mercy: look graciously upon this thy servant, that *he* may be freed from the bands of all bodily infirmity, and by thy merciful favour *his* former health may be renewed; through Jesus Christ our Lord. *Amen.*

SOVEREIGN Lord, our God, Almighty, we beseech thee save us all, thou only Physician of souls and bodies. Sanctify us all, thou that healest every disease; and heal especially this thy servant. Raise *him* up from the bed of pain by thy tender loving-kindness; visit *him* in mercy and compassion; drive away from *him* all sickness and infirmity; that, being raised up by thy mighty Hand, *he* may serve thee with all thankfulness; and that we, being made partakers of thy goodness, may praise and glorify thee, who doest works great and wonderful and worthy to be praised. For it is thine to pity and to save; and to thee we ascribe glory, Father, Son, and Holy Ghost, now and for evermore. *Amen.*

(Greek Office for the Sick. Given in Bright's Ancient Collects.)

2. *For Forgiveness*

(*for the sick person to repeat after the priest*)

MERCIFUL Father, look down upon thy poor sinful child. I am so unworthy, and so weak and helpless, that I scarcely dare to come to thee; yet I have no other help to flee to, and thou art a God of love. Pity me, and forgive me all my miserable failures and infirmities. Lord, I cast myself on thy mercies.

I long to do better. I long to conquer my sins.
I long to make some progress in holiness. Lord,
thou knowest all my desire. Help me by thy
grace to conquer my besetting faults. Make me
meek and gentle and patient and loving to all.
Preserve me from thoughts of self, and self-
seeking. Preserve me from all ill-temper and
unkindliness. Make me bright and helpful and
thoughtful towards others. Above all, give me a
lowly child-like heart, that I may live as thy child
here, and may come to thy glorious home hereafter; through Jesus Christ our Lord. *Amen.*

3. *For Pardon and Cleansing*

O LORD, give me true repentance for the past, and
grant me forgiveness through the merits of thy
well-beloved Son. Lord, thou knowest all my
desire, and my groaning is not hid from thee.
Help me to conquer my besetting sins. Keep me
pure and clean from every thought that can stain
the soul. Help me to grow in grace, and in
knowledge of my Lord and Saviour Jesus Christ.
And when my earthly course is ended, receive me,
unworthy though I be, for the sake of him who
died for my salvation, thy Son Jesus Christ.
Amen.

4. *For the Spirit of Prayer*

O FATHER, have mercy upon thy child, and teach
him to pray. *He* asks of thee the spirit of prayer
and supplication. *His* bodily weakness hindereth

his prayers, so that they are weak and cold and beset by wanderings of mind. Yet *he* longeth to pray; and, Lord, thou knowest all *his* desire, and *his* groaning is not hid from thee. Send thy Holy Spirit to help *his* infirmities, and to teach *him* how to pray. If *he* is weak through the infirmity of the flesh, may that Divine Comforter make intercession for *him*. Teach *him* at least to feel thy presence with *him*, that *he* may look up to thee often, as a child to its father. Let *him* rest in simple trust in thy arms. And, even when he cannot pray to thee as *he* would, may *he* bow beneath *his* cross and never doubt thy love. Accept *him*, O Father, not for *his* own sake, or for the sake of such prayer as *he* offereth, but for the sake only of the merits and intercession of thy dear Son Jesus Christ our Lord. *Amen.*

5. *For a Blessing on Suffering*

O LORD Jesus Christ, who didst bear thy Cross for us, help us to take up our Cross, and to bear it after thee; that so, walking in thy footsteps, and being made like unto thee through suffering, we may attain to thy kingdom, and see thee in thy glory; where, with the Father and the Holy Spirit, thou livest and reignest, ever one God, world without end. *Amen.*

6. *For Strength to Bear the Cross*

O BLESSED Lord Jesus, who didst bear thy Cross for us, give thy feeble children strength to take up their Cross and follow thee. If our Cross be heavy, make us to bear it gladly, that so we may be more like unto thee. Let us not shrink from planting our steps, if need be, in the path of pain in which thou walkedst: for that path will lead us to heaven. Let us not put away from our lips the cup of bitterness which thou drankedst to the dregs: for that bitter cup is life-giving medicine to the soul. We are very weak, but thy strength is made perfect in weakness. May we so suffer with thee here below, that we may rest in thee when we die, and at the last day rise again, in great joy and glory, to reign with thee through endless ages; who livest and reignest with the Father, and the Holy Ghost, one God, world without end. *Amen.*

7. *The Drawing of the Cross*

MERCIFUL Jesus, who wast lifted up from the Cross that thou mightest draw all men unto thee: Have mercy upon thy sinful servants, and draw them closer to thyself through the power of thy blessed Cross. O dear Redeemer, we are still too far from thee. We ask thee with all our hearts to draw us nearer. We would be drawn nearer to thee in *faith*, learning to know better the precious teaching of the Cross. We would be drawn nearer to thee in *likeness*, copying the pattern of thy perfect meekness and patience. Draw us, O merciful Saviour, lifted up from the earth upon the Cross, draw us with the strong cords of thy love; embrace us with the outstretched Arms of thy compassion; and through all trials and temptations, in all times of weakness and danger, keep us close to thee, and suffer us not to go from thee; for thine infinite mercies' sake, who livest and reignest with the Father and the Holy Spirit, one God, world without end. *Amen.*

8. *For the Despondent*

O HOLY Jesu, we fall down before thee, and beseech thee to have mercy upon thine afflicted servant. Lift from *him*, if it might be, the heavy burden of *his* affliction. Thou wast despised and rejected of men, a Man of sorrows, and acquainted with grief. Thou hast borne our griefs, and carried our sorrows. We have not an High Priest which cannot be touched with the feeling of our infirmities. Thou knowest every pain and pang that rends the heart. Thou knowest the heaviness which boweth down thy servant's soul. O thou, whose soul was exceedingly sorrowful, even unto death, look in mercy upon *his* great sorrow. Pardon in *him* all faithless thoughts and fears, and dispel them by thy grace. Lift from above *his* head the dark cloud of despair, and let the bright sunshine of thy love shine round about *him*. Teach *him* to trust thy word and to believe in thy promises, and let *him* not be cast down overmuch by the feelings of *his* own weak and sinful heart. Teach *him* to look from *his* own wounds to thy blessed Cross, and may *he* find healing, and comfort, and peace, as and when thou seest fit. May *he* remember that it is not *his* own feelings but thy promises, which are the pledge of ever-lasting salvation. And, if *he* may not know here joy and peace in believing, may *he* nevertheless enter at length into the joy of *his* Lord, and the perfect peace of Paradise; there to dwell with thee, who livest and reignest, with the Father and the Holy Spirit, one God evermore. *Amen.*

9. *For the Lonely*

O MOST gracious Father, who hast given to thy servant a heavy burden to bear alone; Strengthen *him*, we pray thee, to be able to bear it with humble patience. If it be thy will that *he* should have little earthly comfort and support, fill *his* soul with heavenly consolations: if thou allottest to *him* many long and weary hours of sickness, let *him* feel evermore thy presence with *him*. Teach *him* that *he* is never really alone, since thou art near. Give *him* the power to meditate upon thee, and to spend *his* hours of loneliness in blessed communing with Heaven. May a bright hope gild the clouds of *his* darkest days, and may *he* feel that, though heaviness may endure for a night, yet joy cometh in the morning, even the fulness of joy which is in thy presence for evermore. Hear us, O merciful Father, for the sake of him who was a Man of sorrows and acquainted with grief, our blessed Redeemer, Jesus Christ. *Amen.*

10. *In Great Pain*

O GRACIOUS Father, whose dear Son bore for us unspeakable agonies, being scourged, and crowned with thorns, and nailed to the Cross: Have mercy on thy servant who is now in great suffering, and grant *him* grace to fix *his* eyes upon the Cross, and to find strength there to copy the example of him who, for the joy that was set before him, endured the Cross; that following *his* Divine Master through suffering, *he* may follow him to his eternal glory; through the same thy Son Jesus Christ our Lord. *Amen.*

11. *For One Unable to go to Church*

O HEAVENLY Father, we pray for a blessing upon thy servant hindered by infirmity from going up to the house of prayer. Thine eyes are in every place. Thine ear is open unto prayer that is offered in spirit and truth. Be with thy servant in *his* home, and may *he* find thy presence ever near *him*. Thou hast cut off from *him* the privilege of worshipping with *his* brethren in the congregation. Give *him* much joy and comfort in the prayer that is in secret. And so bless and guide *him*, O merciful Father, that, when the poor imperfect worship of this world is no more, *he* may join for ever in the glorious and perfect worship of the heavenly choirs; through Jesus Christ our Lord. *Amen.*

12. *In Long-Continued Sickness*

O THOU who art the God of patience and consolation: Strengthen this thy servant in the inner man. Lord, *he* is unable to stand under the Cross—unable of *himself*: but thou, O holy Jesus, who didst feel the burden of it, who didst sink under it, and wert pleased to admit a man to bear part of the load, when thou underwentest all for him; be thou pleased to help thy servant to bear this load of pain and sickness, that *he* may be strongest when *he* is weakest, and may be able, through thee strengthening *him*, to do and suffer what thou pleasest. Lord, pity *him*; Lord, sanctify this *his* sickness; Lord, strengthen *him*; Holy Jesus, save and deliver *him*. Thou knowest how often thy servant hath fallen through pleasure: in thy mercy and pity let *him* not fall through pain. Let *him* never offend thee by impatience or an uneasy spirit; but let *him* pass through the valley of tears, the valley of the shadow of death, with safety and peace, with a meek spirit, and a sense of the Divine mercies. Grant this, Eternal God, gracious Father, for the merits and intercessions of our merciful High-Priest, who once suffered for us, and for ever intercedes for us, our most gracious and ever-blessed Saviour Jesus Christ. *Amen.*

13. *For the Aged*

O HEAVENLY Father, who didst bless thine aged servants Simeon and Anna, suffering them to behold with their eyes the Saviour of the world, and to see thy salvation: Bless, we humbly pray thee, this thy servant in *his* latter days. Give *him* a clear knowledge of *his* Saviour, and a sure faith in that Saviour's merits and sacrifice. Let not *his* mind be clouded over with doubts or darkness. May *his* path be as the shining light, which shineth more and more unto the perfect day. May *his* end be calm and blessed. And may *he* pass joyfully from the weakness and weariness of this life to the peace and rest of Paradise; for the sake of Jesus Christ our Lord. *Amen.*

14. *For the Blind*

O JESU, Light of the world, and Sun of righteousness, Look down in mercy upon this thy servant in *his* blindness. Thou camest to give sight to the blind. Give *him*, we pray thee, spiritual sight. Shed the rays of thy blessed truth upon his soul. Enlighten *his* mind to discern clearly the things which belong unto *his* peace. Though the bodily eye be in darkness, may the eye of the soul be full of light. May he have faith to look, not at the things which are seen, but at the things which are not seen. Keep *him* from the darkness of sin and ignorance, from deeds of darkness, and from all dark thoughts. May the light of the glorious Gospel of Jesus Christ shine into *his* soul. May *he* walk as a child of the light. And, when the night of this world is ended, may *he* awake up in thy likeness, and, seeing thee face to face, enter the

43

light of everlasting day. Hear us, O Saviour, who livest and reignest with the Father and the Holy Ghost, one God, world without end. *Amen.*

15. *In Want of Sleep*

O GOD, who art Eternal Light, and in whom is no darkness at all, be with thy servant through the hours of night, and mercifully preserve *him* from all evil; grant unto *him* such quiet and refreshing sleep as may relieve *his* weariness; speak peace unto *his* soul in *his* waking hours, that when awake *he* may watch with Christ, and when sleeping *he* may rest in peace; that waking or sleeping *he* may abide always under thy protection; through Jesus Christ our Lord. *Amen.*

16. *In Fever*

O LORD Jesus Christ, who in the house of thine apostle St. Peter didst heal his wife's mother when sick of a fever: We humbly beseech thee for this thy servant, that thou wouldest mercifully give unto *him* relief, and restoration to health; grant that through thee *he* may drink of the living waters of thy Spirit, and be refreshed with the multitude of thy mercies; who with the Father and the Holy Ghost livest and reignest, ever one God, world without end. *Amen.*

17. *In Great Weakness*

O GOD, the Strength of all them that put their trust in thee, mercifully look upon thy servant, and grant that in *his* bodily weakness *he* may not faint nor be discouraged, but may know assuredly that thou art our Refuge and Strength, a very present help in trouble; and that, though all else fail, yet underneath are the everlasting arms of thine unfailing love. Grant this, O heavenly Father, for Jesus Christ's sake our Lord. *Amen.*

18. *For the Deaf*

O ALMIGHTY Father, who alone canst give consolation and patience to thy children: We humbly pray thee to help thy servant, that, being unable to hear thee by the hearing of the ear, *he* may see thee by faith; and in the silence to which thou hast called *him, he* may yet hear thy voice, and give *his* heart wholly unto thee: grant unto *him* a loving and trustful spirit, that he may in all things seek to do thy will; through Jesus Christ our Lord. *Amen.*

19. *After an Accident*

O GOD, whose never-failing providence ordereth all things both in heaven and earth: Mercifully look upon thy servant; succour and defend *him* from all evil; spare *him* that *he* may recover *his* strength; heal *him* of the injuries *he* has suffered; and grant that in all the changes and chances of this mortal life, his heart may surely there be fixed where true joys are to be found; through Jesus Christ our Lord. *Amen.*

20. *Before an Operation*

LORD of all power and might, we humbly beseech thee to look down in mercy on this thy servant; strengthen *him* both in body and soul, that *he* may commit *himself* into thy hands in perfect trust. Grant that what is now about to be done may be effectual to the healing of *his* body, and serve to the benefit of *his* soul. Give wisdom and skill to those who attend upon *him*, and grant that through the merits of thy dear Son *he* may have perfect peace and safety; through the same thy Son Jesus Christ our Lord. *Amen.*

21. *After an Operation*

ALMIGHTY God, who art the Giver of all good things: Look mercifully upon this thy servant, and grant that what has been now done may by thy help be brought to a successful issue. Give *him* grace to bear patiently whatever pain or weariness *he* may have to endure: restore *him* to *his* bodily health, if it be thy gracious will; and grant that *he* may so pass through things temporal that *he* finally lose not the things eternal. Hear us, O heavenly Father, and answer us according to the multitude of thy mercies; through Jesus Christ, our Lord. *Amen.*

22. *For Nervous Sufferers*

O BLESSED Jesus, who didst speak peace to the troubled waters, and didst reassure thy affrighted

46

disciples: Look mercifully upon this thy servant. Deliver *him* from all troubled and unquiet thoughts; perfect thy strength in *his* weakness, and grant that in patience *he* may possess *his* soul by leaning only on the help of thy heavenly grace. Help *him* to stay *his* mind on thee, that, trusting in thee, *he* may be kept in thy perfect peace, now and ever. *Amen.*

23. *For One with Mind Clouded*

ALMIGHTY and everliving God, who by thy holy apostle hast taught us to pray for one another, and especially for those who cannot pray for themselves: We beseech thee to hear our prayer for this our *brother* in *his* weakness and helplessness. Mercifully drive away the clouds which obscure *his* understanding, and grant that *he* may be enabled to receive thy holy Word, and to turn to thee in true penitence and faith. Restore to *him* the power of self-control, that *he* may offer unto thee the sacrifice of praise and thanksgiving, to the glory of thy Name, through Jesus Christ our Lord. *Amen.*

24. *With the Friends of One Wandering in Mind*

O GRACIOUS Father, we commend to thy great mercy this our afflicted *brother*. It hath pleased thee to take from *him* the power to pray. Hear, we beseech thee, the unworthy prayers of thy servants who make intercession for *him*. Magnify thy mercy in forgiving one who cannot seek forgiveness. Grant unto *him* all things needful for *him*. We know not whether thou wilt be pleased to restore to *him* the blessing of a conscious mind in this world. Be it as thou wilt, not as we will; but may *he* wake in the next world to a glorious resurrection and know even as he is known. Grant this through Jesus Christ our Lord. *Amen.*

25. *For those who Attend on the Sick*

MERCIFUL Lord, we beseech thee to strengthen and support thy servants who are called to tend the sufferer and to watch beside the bed of sickness. Give them grace to fulfil their task with patient endurance and with loving tenderness. Comfort them in their weariness with the comfort of thy blessed Spirit. May this season of self-denying labour be a season of much spiritual welfare to their own souls. May they learn to seek the things above, and to choose the one thing needful, while health and strength are given them, and ever to commit themselves into thy hands to do with them and through them what thou wilt, through Jesus Christ our Lord. *Amen.*

26. *For Blessing on the Means Used*

O ALMIGHTY God, who by thy Holy Spirit givest wisdom and understanding to thy children: We humbly beseech thee to bless and direct the means which are used for the recovery of thy servant, and make them so effectual to that end, that *he* may be restored to health, if it be thy gracious will; through Jesus Christ our Lord. *Amen.*

27. *For Doctors and Nurses*

O MERCIFUL Father, who hast wonderfully fashioned man in thine own image, and hast made his body to be a temple of the Holy Ghost: Sanctify, we beseech thee, all those whom thou hast called to study and practise the arts of healing the sick, and the prevention of disease and pain. Strengthen them in body and soul, and bless their work, that they may themselves live as members and servants of Christ, and give comfort to those whom he lived and died to save; through him who now liveth and reigneth with thee in the unity of the Holy Ghost, one God, world without end. *Amen.*

V. A FORM OF THANKSGIVING FOR RECOVERY

To be repeated after the priest.

Glory be to thee, O heavenly Father, for all thy mercies to me. Before I was troubled I went wrong: but now will I keep thy word. It is good for me that I have been in trouble, that I may learn thy statutes.

I called upon the Lord in trouble, and the Lord heard me at large.

O what great troubles and adversities hast thou showed me, and yet didst thou turn and refresh

49

me, yea, and broughtest me from the deep of the earth again.

Praised be the Lord daily, even the God which helpeth us and poureth his benefits upon us.

Glory be to the Father, and to the Son: and to the Holy Ghost; As it was in the beginning, is now, and ever shall be: world without end. *Amen*.

Praise the Lord, O my soul: and all that is within me praise his holy Name.

In partial Recovery

GREAT and mighty God, who bringest down to the grave, and bringest up again: We bless thy wonderful goodness for having turned our heaviness into joy, and our mourning into gladness, by restoring this our *brother* to some degree of *his* former health. Blessed be thy Name that thou didst not forsake *him* in *his* sickness; but didst visit *him* with comforts from above; didst support *him* in patience and submission to thy will; and at last didst send *him* seasonable relief. Perfect, we beseech thee, this thy mercy towards *him ;* and prosper the means which shall be made use of for *his* cure; that, being restored to health of body, vigour of mind, and cheerfulness of spirit, *he* may be able to go to thy house, to offer thee an oblation with great gladness, and to bless thy holy Name for all thy goodness towards *him*; through Jesus Christ our Saviour, to whom, with thee and the Holy Spirit, be all honour and glory, world without end. *Amen*.

In fuller Recovery

O most gracious and loving Father, we humbly fall down before thee, and render unto thee our heartfelt thanks for thy great mercy to this thy servant, in raising *him* up from the bed of sickness, and granting *him* the blessing of renewed health and strength. We are not worthy of the least of thy mercies, yet thou pourest thy benefits upon us; glory to thy Name! For all temporal mercies to thy servant—for removal of danger, for ease of pain, for restoration to those near and dear to *him*—we bless thee and praise thee, O Father. But yet more for all spiritual blessings and mercies—for the precious lessons of the sick-bed, for the refining fire of trouble and suffering. O Lord, we thank thee: help our unthankfulness. Make us more thankful for thy great and undeserved mercies, and more deserving of them; through Jesus Christ our dear Redeemer. *Amen.*

Then shall be said these verses, or else the whole of Psalm 103.

Praise the Lord, O my soul: and forget not all his benefits;

Who forgiveth all thy sin: and healeth all thine infirmities;

Who saveth thy life from destruction: and crowneth thee with mercy and loving-kindness.

Glory be to the Father, and to the Son: and to the Holy Ghost;

51

As it was in the beginning, is now, and ever shall be: world without end. *Amen.*

Also Psalms 116 *and* 138.

O LORD and heavenly Father, we cannot render due thanks and praise for all thy mercies bestowed upon us. Yet we beseech thee to accept these our unworthy prayers and praises which we offer unto thy divine Majesty, for thy great goodness and loving-kindness which thou hast showed unto thy servant. Preserve in *his* soul, O God, a constant and clear sense of thy mercies, that *he* may make a complete and entire surrender of *himself* to thy service; that *he* may always praise thee faithfully here on earth, until it shall please thee to call *him* nearer to the place of thy heavenly habitation, to praise thee eternally; through Jesus Christ our Lord. *Amen.*

OUR Father, which art in heaven, Hallowed be thy Name. Thy kingdom come. Thy will be done, in earth as it is in heaven. Give us this day our daily bread. And forgive us our trespasses, As we forgive them that trespass against us. And lead us not into temptation; But deliver us from evil; For thine is the kingdom, the power and the glory, for ever and ever. *Amen.*

Glory be to the Father of mercies, the Father of men and angels, the Father of our Lord Jesus Christ.

Glory be to the most holy and eternal Son of

God, the blessed Saviour and redeemer of the world.

Glory be to the holy and eternal Spirit of God, the Comforter, the sanctifying and life-giving Spirit.

All glory and thanks, all honour and power, all love and obedience, be unto the most holy, blessed, and undivided Trinity, now, henceforth, and for ever. *Amen.*

The priest will naturally show the Holy Eucharist to be the highest form of thanksgiving, in order to lead to its use as such.

THE INSTRUCTION OF THE SICK

I. THE BIBLE

(a) *Suggestions for using the Bible*

1. With older folk, who may be presumed to know parts at least of the Bible, use, if possible, some passage which is clearly familiar. For in sickness the effort to take in something new may be too great, whereas memories can be awakened by something known in the past.

2. A test may be made by asking if there is any special passage which the sick man would like read. But this must not be our rule, for the passage should be decided on beforehand, and carefully studied, with the thought of a prayer or thanksgiving to be based on it and offered after reading.

3. With younger folk we cannot take any knowledge of the words of Scripture for granted. The only familiar part may be the Gospel. Our Lord's works of healing can always be used. Thought should be directed, not to the wonder of a miracle long ago, but to the certainty that he still wills the healing of those who turn to him for help.

4. A few words of comfort should always be given, if possible both before and after the reading.

5. The teaching of the Gospel story must not be separated from what has resulted from it—the teaching and practice, sacramental and otherwise, of the Church. For instance, the healing of the

paralytic may be shown as teaching that healing of the soul must be sought first; the story of the Last Supper may be used to introduce an invitation to the receiving of Communion; and the Mission of the Twelve in St. Mark ch. 6 may lead to a few words on Holy Unction. And the Prodigal Son may show, not only the blessedness of repentance, but also the true character of God, which may correct many mistaken ideas of him.

6. In chronic cases we may use some faithful layman or woman for the regular reading of the Bible, going ourselves to take the message further and offer the Church's help more definitely.

7. The sick man must not think that the priest ignores the Bible, and our use of it with him may best consist in reading some brief passage, perhaps only a verse or two. In this way we can repeat it more than once, trying to fix it in the sufferer's mind, and giving him some words which he may repeat to himself afterwards.

8. There are many books which suggest the choice of passages or verses for reading. A useful list is given at the end of the " Visitation of the Sick " in the 1928 Prayer Book. The *St. Raphael Prayer Book for the Sick* (S.P.C.K.) gives a list of brief passages or verses arranged under twelve headings. The same book gives a series of thanksgivings suggested by words from the Psalms. It need not be added that the Psalms supply material for much besides thanksgiving.

9. It is often good to leave with the sick man

some words in the form of an "affirmation", which may be repeated often by him. For this the words of Scripture are the best. They may be from the Psalms, such as "Though I am sometime afraid: yet put I my trust in thee" (Ps. 56. 3). And there are many to be found in the words of S. Paul, such as Rom. 8. 35–39; Phil. 4. 13; 2 Tim. 1. 12.

10. It is unhappily the case that some households do not possess a Bible. If we ask for a Bible and one is not to be had, it may be an excuse for leaving one (which need not be a new one) at our next visit. Also some member of the family may be asked to read to the patient, and should be instructed what to read. This may lead to a new knowledge and use of the Bible in such a household.

(b) *Lists of Passages for Reading*

1. *The Psalms*

The Psalms form a treasury of their own, and are therefore given first. The following thirty-five psalms are placed under several headings.

Penitence and Forgiveness.

> Psalm   6. O Lord, rebuke me not.
>
>   32. Blessed is he whose unrighteousness is forgiven.
>
>   51. Have mercy upon me, O God.
>
>   130. Out of the deep have I called upon thee.
>
>   143. Hear my prayer, O Lord.

Encouragement

Psalm 13. How long wilt thou forget me,
O Lord.

16. Preserve me, O God.

18. I will love thee, O Lord, my
strength (*verses* 1–6 *and* 18–
32).

91. Whoso dwelleth under the defence of the most High.

121. I will lift up mine eyes unto the
hills.

In Despondency

Psalm 22. My God, my God, look upon
me.

38. Put me not to rebuke, O Lord.

42. Like as the hart desireth the
water-brooks.

86. Bow down thine ear, O Lord.

In Pain or Trouble

Psalm 46. God is our refuge and strength.

69. Save me, O God (*verses* 1–3,
13–18, 30–37).

77. I will cry unto God with my
voice.

88. O Lord God of my salvation.

142. I cried unto the Lord with my
voice.

143. Hear my prayer, O Lord.

E

When near Death

> Psalm 23. The Lord is my Shepherd.
> 25. Unto thee, O Lord, will I lift up my soul.
> 27. The Lord is my light, and my salvation.

Praise and Thanksgiving

> Psalm 34. I will alway gives thanks unto the Lord.
> 40. I waited patiently for the Lord.
> 63. O God, thou art my God.
> 103. Praise the Lord, O my soul.
> 145. I will magnify thee, O God, my King.

Also in special thanksgiving for recovery

> Psalm 30. I will magnify thee, O Lord.
> 116. I am well pleased.
> 138. I will give thanks unto thee, O Lord.

General

> Psalm 23. The Lord is my Shepherd.
> 31. In thee, O Lord, have I put my trust.
> 61. Hear my crying, O God.
> 71. In thee, O Lord, have I put my trust.
> 84. O how amiable are thy dwellings.

2. *Passages of Scripture for Reading with the Sick*

At the end of *Pastor in Parochia* (pp. 349–464) as many as one hundred and twenty-two such passages are given in full. There is not space in this book to give so many, or to print them in full. The following is a very much shorter selection, ten from the Old Testament and forty-five from the New.

(a) *The Old Testament*

Deut. 30. 11–20. The pleading of Moses for the choice of life and good.

1 Sam. 12. 20–25. Samuel's exhortation as to God's mercy and faithfulness.

Isa. 26. 1–9. The blessedness of trust in God.

Isa. 38. Hezekiah's sickness and prayer.

Isa. 40. 1–11. The prophecy of the coming of Christ.

Isa. 52. 13–53. 12. The prophecy of the Atonement.

Isa. 55. 1–3, 6–13. God's gracious invitation.

Lam. 3. 17–27. Trust in God in affliction.

Dan. 9. 3–19. Daniel's confession and prayer.

Mic. 6. 1–8. God's pleading with his people.

(b) *The New Testament*

Matt. 5. 1–12. The Beatitudes.

Matt. 6. 25–34. Trust in God.

Matt. 18. 21–35. The unmerciful servant.

Matt. 22. 1–14. The Marriage Feast.

Matt. 25. 1–13. The ten Virgins.

Matt. 26. 36–46. Gethsemane.

Mark 2. 1–12. The Sick of the Palsy.

Mark 5. 22–43. Jairus' daughter, and the woman in the crowd.

Mark 6. 7–13. The healing work of the disciples.

Mark 7. 32–37. The deaf man of Decapolis.

Mark 9. 14–29. The epileptic Boy.

Mark 10. 46–52. Blind Bartimaeus.

Luke 2. 25–35. Simeon.

Luke. 10. 38–42. Martha and Mary.

Luke 12. 16–31. The rich Fool.

Luke 15. 1–10. The lost sheep and the lost coin.

Luke 15. 11–24. The Prodigal Son.

Luke 17. 11–19. The ten Lepers.

Luke 22. 14–20. The institution of the Eucharist.

Luke 23. 33–46. The Crucifixion.

Luke 36–47. The Resurrection.

John 3. 14–21. God's purpose in Redemption.

John 6. 47–58. The Bread of Life.

John 11. 20–27. Assurance of the Resurrection.

John 14. 1–26. Christ is the Way.

John 15. 1–10. The Vine and the Branches.

John 20. 11–18. Mary Magdalene and the Risen Christ.

Acts 3. 1–10. The lame man at the temple gate.

Acts 9. 32–42. St. Peter's healing ministry.

Acts 28. 7–10. St. Paul's healing ministry.

Rom. 5. 1–11. The fruits of God's mercy.

Rom. 8. 14–39. Christian assurance.

1 Cor. 15. 50–58. The hope of resurrection.

2 Cor. 4. 14–5. 10.   The things temporal and things eternal.

Eph. 6. 10–20.   The armour of God.

Phil. 3. 7–14.   Losing all and gaining Christ.

1 Thess. 5. 1–11.   Watchfulness.

Heb. 4. 14–16, and 7. 24–27.   Our great High Priest.

Jas. 5. 13–18.   Healing and prayer in the Church.

1 Pet. 2. 20–25.   Christ's example in suffering.

1 John 3. 1–8.   The Christian Hope.

1 John 4. 9–21.   God's love to man.

Rev. 7. 9–17.   Heaven and its worship.

Rev. 21. 1–7.   The new Heaven and Earth.

Rev. 22. 1–7.   Before the Throne of God.

3. *Affirmations*

(*Passages taken from Scripture, to be given to the sick man to say over and over again in moments of need*)

Exod. 33. 14.   My presence shall go with thee, and I will give thee rest.

Josh. 1. 18.   Only be strong and of good courage.

Ps. 27. 16.   O tarry thou the Lord's leisure: be strong, and He shall comfort thine heart; and put thou thy trust in the Lord.

Ps. 73. 25.   My flesh and my heart faileth: but God is the strength of my heart, and my portion for ever.

Ps. 108. 28.   Thou art my God, and I will thank thee: thou art my God, and I will praise thee.

Isa. 26. 3.   Thou wilt keep him in perfect peace,

whose mind is stayed on thee: because he trusteth in thee.

Jer. 17. 14. Heal me, O Lord, and I shall be healed; save me, and I shall be saved; for thou art my praise.

Of the many suitable verses in the New Testament, the following are a few.

Mark 5. 36. Fear not, only believe.

Mark 9. 24. I believe; help thou mine unbelief.

Mark 14. 36. Father, all things are possible unto thee; remove this cup from me: howbeit not what I will, but what thou wilt.

Luke 1. 38. Behold the handmaid of the Lord; be it unto me according to thy word.

John 14. 1. Let not your heart be troubled: ye believe in God, believe also in me.

John 16. 33. In the world ye shall have tribulation: but be of good cheer. I have overcome the world.

Acts 4. 12. There is none other Name under heaven given among men whereby we must be saved.

Rom. 8. 35, 37. Who can separate us from the love of Christ? Shall tribulation or anguish? . . . Nay, in all these things we are more than conquerors through him that loved us.

1 Cor. 10. 13. God is faithful, who will not suffer you to be tempted above that ye are able.

Phil. 4. 13. I can do all things through Christ which strengtheneth me.

2 Tim. 1. 12.   I know him whom I have believed, and I am persuaded that he is able to guard that which I have committed unto him against that day.

2 Tim. 4. 18.   The Lord will deliver me from every evil work, and will save me unto his heavenly kingdom.

1 John 4. 18.   There is no fear in love: but perfect love casteth out fear.

Rev. 1. 17, 18.   Fear not; I am the first and the last and the Living one; and I was dead, and behold, I am alive for evermore, and I have the keys of death and Hades.

Rev. 21. 4.   God shall wipe away every tear from their eyes; and death shall be no more; neither shall there be mourning, nor crying, nor pain, any more.

To these passages should be added the Comfortable Words, *which for the faithful will already have such sacred associations.*

II. TALKS IN ACUTE SICKNESS

(a) *General Considerations*

In visiting cases of acute sickness, the priest may need to be reminded of sundry preliminaries.

In many cases he has only access to the sick man by the permission of the doctor and the nurse. Both of them have therefore to be considered. If the nurse refuses admission because the doctor has ordered that no one should visit his patient, it is best for the priest to ring up the doctor and get his permission. If it is not given readily, let him express his readiness to obey his wishes with regard to time and length of visit, and point out that in his spiritual province he is offering himself to help in the process of healing, going to the patient to cheer and encourage, and not to alarm or depress him. If it is not easy to get into touch with the doctor, let him ask the nurse to speak about it to the doctor at his next visit, so that an exception may be made in the case of the priest who brings spiritual help.

If it is for the patient's sake that the nurse or relative may hesitate, let him assure them that it will be a quiet and cheering visit, lasting only five minutes (or ten, if this is allowed), and then let him keep strictly to the limit stated.

The following suggestions are made with regard to the actual visit:

1. There is no need to waste time in asking the sick man about his illness. (It is best to ask someone else first.) Nor should he begin with any secular talk. The priest should be priest at once. He can show this by saying " The Lord be with you " as he approaches the bed.

2. In acute sickness no patient is at his best. He is not likely to be receptive of what is new. In grave illness words such as those of familiar hymns will reach him best, and the Lord's Prayer. Then a few words should follow, said very quietly

and slowly, the priest perhaps holding his hand. The talk should lead to prayer, which should include some simple extempore words, and always conclude with a blessing.

3. It is before the final blessing that the laying on of hands may well be given, either formally, as a special act for which the sick man has been prepared, or as an informal act, during which the priest silently offers himself to be the channel of our Lord's healing grace. (See pp. 22–33 for such use of the ministry of healing.)

4. If the sick man is ready to talk, encourage him to do so, leading him to speak of his spiritual state. Now is the time to tell him of penitence as a condition of forgiveness, and the joy of the assurance that his sins are forgiven. But he should not be hurried into an act of confession, unless his end is near. That may wait till the next day. And he must not be frightened about it. Leave him with some words to say over to himself. If he is likely to know the words, let them be " If we confess our sins, He is faithful and just, etc.". Or else a familiar verse such as " He died that we might be forgiven, etc."

5. Return if possible the next day, if his life is in danger, and begin at once with *repentance*. This will need a talk, or more than one, such as are suggested under the " Talks " which follow, and they must vary according to his spiritual state. Give him absolution if he is prepared for it. Meanwhile *faith* must have its place, as well as

repentance. Say the Creed, perhaps asking him to repeat it with you, or to say after it, "All this I steadfastly believe".

If he is a communicant, talk of the Blessed Sacrament, and arrange to bring it to him, using Reservation when possible, and thus making the service a short one.

6. After his Communion, tell him of Holy Unction, and prepare him for it, if he is ready and willing to receive it. His family should be told about this, and it will probably need to be explained to them too. Let them be invited to be present at the anointing, to help with their prayers for wholeness both of body and soul. They should be taught throughout that *their* attitude of expectant faith will make a real difference to his chance of recovery.

7. If death is imminent, follow the line of *Prayers for the Dying* (pp. 111–116), and remember that prayer will often reach those who are apparently unconscious. If there is any betterment, encourage the least sign of it, and lead him to thanksgiving, making him repeat such words as the opening verses of Psalm 103. In later stages of recovery help him to see that he must show his thankfulness by a fuller practice of a Christian's life and duties.

The above suggestions are of a general kind. What has been said about repentance and confession supposes that the illness is so grave that there is no time to spare. But in many cases of sickness which may be called " acute " there is time for fuller teaching and ministrations. The suggestions in the outlines of the " Talks " which follow are meant as a help in this direction.

(b) *On Repentance and Confession*

1. *With one who has little idea of his own sinfulness.*

(a) The sick man may prove to have no sense of sin, owing to his having held wrong ideas of religion all his life. He will say that he has led a better life than many, has never done anyone any harm, etc. Something must be done first to convince him of sin, and yet, if he is very ill, it must be done with real gentleness. Remind him of what was pledged at his baptism, and ask if his life has been a following of that of Jesus. Explain to him that sins are of omission as well as commission, and against God as well as against man. Tell him that not to feel a sense of sin is a very bad sign. Remind him that even S. Paul felt himself to be the chief of sinners. Then speak to him of your own sense of sin, and the comfort and joy of knowing that it was sinners that Christ came to save. Kneel down and make a simple act of sorrow for sin and for the blindness of not feeling it, coupling yourself with him in what you say. Begin it by saying, " If we say that we have no sin, etc.".

(b) At the next visit take it for granted that he now has some sense of sin. Tell him you are going to read him the most encouraging story in the world, in which our Lord told us what a man must do when he realizes his sin, and what God will do. Read the story of the Prodigal Son from St. Luke 15. 11–32. Remind him that the son knew what he had done wrong and confessed it, and then pray that the Holy Spirit may show him where *he* has sinned, and that he may really be sorry, and that he may have the courage to bring it up to the surface and confess it and receive God's forgiving welcome.

(*c*) At a third visit he may perhaps be led (very gently) to tell of something done wrong in the past. Make this a starting-point, but tell him that though it seems the chief thing in his own eyes, it may not be in God's eyes, and there must be much besides. Suggest to him various ways in which he may still in the present not be faithful to Christ, perhaps encouraging him by mentioning some of your own temptations. Where he responds, jot it down, and then, when it comes to the actual confession, help him out by reminding him of the points. Say over to him first the words of confession (as in the *Visitation of the Sick* in the 1928 Prayer Book), and also tell him the words (from the Prayer Book Service) in which you are going to absolve him, so that he may be prepared beforehand for what is coming (see p. 11). Try to feel something of the " joy in heaven over one sinner that repenteth ", and make him feel it too. And if he recovers, he must not be allowed to go back, but such spiritual touch must be maintained that he may remain a faithful penitent.

If no impression is made by any efforts of the kind suggested above, do not give up hope, but show your continued care of him, praying daily for his conversion, and telling him that you are doing so.

It may be that he has a rooted objection to sacramental confession, perhaps due to teaching and influence early in life. This may have to be overcome, but *not by argument*, which may only increase his bodily sickness and mental distress. You may have to be content with a general act of repentance on his part. If you think it is genuine, accept it as such, tell him that you are going to pronounce God's forgiveness, and do it in the words of the Absolution in the Holy Communion Office.

2. *With one whose sense of sinfulness is inhibited.*

There are some who give at first the impression that they have no sense of sin, which therefore can be awakened only gradually. But really it is simply buried, and below their conscious mind. Careful watch must be made to see if this is the case, and you should never be without hope that an apparently callous man may need something to break down inhibition. There are cases where the recalling of the religion of his childhood may have this effect. A man with no apparent desire for repentance has been known to burst into tears during the repeating of the 51st Psalm, after first making the encouraging remark, " That was my mother's favourite psalm ". Some knowledge of at least the elements of psychology is needed in dealing with such cases.

3. *With a regular churchgoer.*

When a man is a frequenter of the House of God, he will know and use the public confessions in the Prayer Book. It may be well to begin by helping him to make use of them. Then he should be told that the Church has special care for its sick members, and further help in bringing them to God. Open the Prayer Book at the Visitation of the Sick, and read him the words bidding you to move him to make a *special* confession of his sins, and repeat the words of God's forgiveness which follow. Read him the story of the paralytic in St. Matt. 9. 1–8, showing him that our Lord first healed his soul with " thy sins are forgiven ", and then could add the healing of the body with the words, "Arise and walk ". Tell him that you want to help him to this. If he thinks that it was only our Lord himself who had this power, read him the words in S. John 20. 22, 23, where he passed it on to those who were to be shepherds of his flock, and add the words in the Ordination of a priest, reminding him that they were spoken to yourself. But the idea of all this may be altogether too new to be grasped by one in grave illness. So, though he should " be moved to make a special confession of his sins ", he must not be worried into it, nor made to think that the general confession and absolution already used are of no avail.

If he has ever used Confession before, even if it were only as a boy before his Confirmation, it is much easier to help him, and he should be asked whether this is the case.

A sick man must never be urged to the healing of his soul with a view to the healing of his body, but when true penitence is present, he may be told that he may look for the peace that enters his soul through forgiveness to promote the well-being of his mind and body too. If Holy Unction is to be given, it should always be preceded by a definite act of Confession, and when the Laying-on-of-Hands is given in a formal way, it is there also the best form of preparation, though of course it is far more than that.

(c) *On Preparation for Death.*

This subject is dealt with fully on pp. 108–116. But it is closely linked with this section also, and the following are put forward as " General Considerations " in such ministry.

In itself this subject is one that one Christian man ought to have no difficulty in talking about to another. But there are many considerations to be taken into account, which vary in different cases. It may be well to enumerate them.

1. If the priest has gained access to the patient

on the understanding that he is a helper of the doctor in the healing process, to suggest the coming of death may seem like a betrayal of trust, for it is likely to rob the patient of some of that hopefulness of recovery which is one of the aids towards attaining it. It may be possible to consult the doctor in the matter, but it must be remembered that the point of view of the medical profession is different from that of the Church. Doctors and nurses hesitate to speak openly of death being imminent as long as there is a shred of hope of recovery.

2. Apart from the doctor, the sick man himself must be considered, and the subject must be introduced so gently that, rather than the giving up of hope, a spiritual hope must be introduced to take the place of the earthly one. Here the language of the Collect in the *Communion of the Sick* may be a guide, which prays " that he may recover his bodily health (if it be thy gracious will); and whensoever his soul shall depart from the body, it may be without spot presented unto thee ". The use of such prayers will put the thought gently, and may lead to a subsequent talk, possibly begun by himself. If he is led first to repentance and confession, his outlook will already have been changed with regard to the meaning of life and death. Often he will have already fully realized the meaning of death without speaking of it, and will be thankful for the chance to face it openly with the help of his priest.

3. There is also the sick man's family to be considered. It may be necessary to give a talk to them also, leading them to see that it would be wrong to let their dear one pass unknowing to the other side when there is time to prepare him. It is not good that the first they should hear of it is for him to say, when the priest has gone, and they return to the sick-room, " He thinks I'm going to die ".

4. The reaction to the thought of death varies greatly. Bacon's words are to some extent true of all, " Men fear death as children fear to go into the dark ". But sometimes callous natures face it boldly and calmly, while the more highly strung, however faithfully they have lived the Christian life, are terrified of it. The priest's aim is to show it as a going not into the dark, but into the light.

5. At the same time it is the priest's plain duty to prepare his people for death, and he must beware of allowing considerations such as the above to excuse him from it or delay it unduly. And yet all the time it must be remembered that " preparation for death " is not a particular ministry with a special technique. If the best preparation for death is a good life, *all* his ministrations will have had in view a readiness to pass into the Presence, and certainly " preparation " does not begin when the sick man is told that death is near. Many of the most beautiful and Christian deaths are of those who have made no last-moment preparation for it, and often the weakening of the faculties makes that impossible.

III. INSTRUCTION IN LONG SICKNESS

(a) *General Considerations*

A few considerations are here set forth which should be taken into account by those fulfilling this part of their ministry.

1. In visiting cases of long-continued sickness, the priest is beset by two opposite dangers, (*a*) of giving too much of his time to one invalid to the detriment of others ; (*b*) of getting tired of the case or feeling that there is not any more that he can say or do.

(*a*) The first difficulty may be solved by getting some devout member of the congregation to undertake a regular weekly visit, which will not be a short one, but will consist of a chat, some reading of the Bible, hymns, etc., and sometimes preparation for a priestly visit, such as instruction in how to make a Confession, or help in preparing for a Communion. The priest's visits will be less frequent, and he will go, not as a friend to chat, but as a priest to minister, only staying longer when there seems more to be done. He should himself give some guidance about passages to be read from the Bible.

(*b*) There must be some system in the ministry given, which should be thought out beforehand. And there must be something more than a course of instruction. The sick man is in a groove, in body and in spirit. He needs to be lifted out of it, at least in spirit. There should be expectation that this will come about, which he should be made to share. It may prove to be a step towards bodily betterment; false hopes should not be raised, but he should be taught not to think of himself as " incurable ".

2. The average Churchman still needs much instruction in the faith, and many of our folk know nothing at all about the Church and its teaching. Sickness gives an opportunity for a course of instruction. This may well be along the lines laid down in some book, and there are many cases in which the book may be put into the hands of the person visited. Such instruction must lead from doctrine to practice, and link one with the other, leading not only to a fuller church life, but also to a fuller life in Christ.

3. He must be taught to pray. All our people need more help in this than we give them, and here is an opportunity. He must learn that he can make his time of enforced leisure a time of helping our Lord and his Church and people by Intercession, and that this cannot be an isolated act, but must be part of a wider system of worship and devotion. And he must be linked with others, by some such means as the forming of a band of intercessors among the chronic invalids of the parish.

4. These regular visits will bring the priest into touch with the rest of the household. Such an *entrée* may be used to help them too.

5. The priest, as a faithful dispenser of the sacraments as well as of the word, will lead up to sacramental teaching and practice as his constant aim. If the sick man has not been confirmed, he will aim at preparing him for it. The lapsed communicant should be gently led back to a regular receiving of the Sacrament. Sickness is a time, as the Prayer Book plainly urges, for hearing about the Sacrament of Absolution, and learning to make a Confession, which may well lead to the Laying-on-of-Hands, and in many cases to the Sacrament of Holy Unction. If another priest has laid a foundation, find out what it is, and build upon it.

6. It must be remembered that no one fixed plan will suit all cases. Sick folk are at all the various stages of the Christian life, and also differ in knowledge, intelligence, and capacity for spiritual things. We must adapt our methods to each case, though there must always be an aim and a plan.

7. The ministry of healing must not be denied because the case seems to be " chronic ". Divine Healing is for mind and spirit as well as for the body, and a higher " healing " may come without a physical " cure ". But those who use this ministry can testify that no case of sickness is of too long standing for restoration by such means.

Often when material means have failed, spiritual means may have an effect on one part of the personality which permeates the whole. The priest should be aware that there are cases of long sickness where the unconscious mind of the invalid has become attached to the condition in which he or she (if the word " she " is used it is because this is a more common effect on women than on men) has become the centre of the little world of the household. The conscious mind may be longing for a renewal of health and normal life, but the inner mind shrinks from losing what has become so precious. The invalid would be indignant at being told that she does not get well because there is a part of her which does not want it. Yet she must see that for herself before healing can begin. The suggestion must be conveyed gradually and gently, perhaps by describing such a mental condition in general terms as that of *some* invalids, and leaving her to think for a while whether it applies to herself.

8. Last, but not least, it must always be remembered that, although pain and suffering are in themselves a sad result of this fallen world, they may cease to be an evil and become a good by being given to God for his glory and the help of our fellows. There are sufferers in whom their very pains may mean an advance in the spiritual life. S. Paul's words in Col. 1. 24, " I fill up that which is behind of the afflictions of Christ in my flesh for his body's sake, which is the Church ",

may form the text from which the sufferer may be led to a conscious union of his sufferings with those of his crucified Lord, and to a sense that, in the fellowship of Christ's Body the Church, he may offer his sufferings as a reparation for the sins both of the Church and of the world. This is a great subject, which cannot be adequately dealt with here. But reference may be made to that well-known book, *The Problem of Pain*, by G. E. Childs, which has been of help to many sufferers. The thought of Reparation is also briefly treated in a small book, *The Problem of Suffering : Towards a Solution*, by A. O. Barkway.

(b) *On the Christian Faith*

(*The following outline talks are based upon the Creed*)

1. *God.*

The sick man might be hostile to the idea of talks on dogmatic theology, but he is sure to respond to the invitation, " Let us talk about God ". Tell him some of man's mistaken ideas about God, and, if he can be led to give his own ideas, show where they are also wrong. Then talk of the nature of God, and, starting perhaps with the fact that " God is Love ", show that eternal love must be reciprocal, and implies eternal Persons in the Godhead. So love does not start with man, but with God, and there can be no question (such as sickness sometimes suggests) of " Can he be a loving God ? " We must look for God's love and expect it. Finally, turn his thoughts, and then his prayers, to thankfulness for this Divine love, and to our life as meant to be a response to it. God's relation to the world of Nature may be illustrated by reading Psalm 104, and to the world of men by reading Psalm 103.

2. *Man.*

Begin with creation as intended to be the response to God's love—the unconscious response in Nature, leading to the conscious response in man, made in God's image. But it must not be a forced response, or it is meaningless. A test is needed, a choice of good or evil. Evil was already in existence, and the devil allowed to test man by temptation. Man turned away from God. This is what is meant by *sin*. Lead the sick man along these lines to a confession of his disloyalty to God, both for all men and also for himself. Read Psalms 8 and 50.

3. *Redemption.*

God the Son became man, in order to give as man the response to the Father's love which he had given already as God, and mankind had hopelessly failed to give. His offering of himself on the Cross was that man's sin might be done away. The way of salvation through union with him is offered to all. Read 2 Cor. 5. 14–21.

4. *Salvation*

The Christian is more than a follower of Christ. By baptism he becomes in a new sense a son of the

Father, as an adopted son made one with the true and eternal Son. He is thus united to the ascended Christ in newness of life. Read Rom. 6. 1–14.

5. *The Holy Spirit*

Speak of this Person within the Godhead, his work in the world as " the Lord and giver of life ", and his giving inner life from the day of Pentecost onwards to the Church, the Body of Christ on earth. Show how he works most definitely in the Sacraments of the Church. If the sick man has not been confirmed, this may lead him to the desire for it. Read Rom. 8. 11–17.

6. *The Church*

As a member of Christ, each Christian is a member of a body, and that body is the Church. It is a fellowship, the family of God. Union with Christ means union with each other. But the Church is not a society of Christian people in contrast with the rest of the world. It has been called " the expeditionary force of the Kingdom of God ". The first duty of the Church and of all its members is to continue the work which the Saviour began, and bring the whole world nearer to Him. It seeks to advance " the Kingdom of God " both in our own street and parish and to the ends of the earth. Its marching orders are, " Go ye into all the world and make disciples of all the nations, baptizing them into the Name of the Father and of the Son and of the Holy Ghost ". The Church militant here in earth is only a very small part of the whole Church. The words added in the Creed, "The Communion of Saints", show us that we are part of a fellowship which includes also the Church Expectant in Paradise (that state of waiting for further blessedness in which the faithful departed of all ages are now living), and the Church Triumphant in heaven, that glorious company of the greatest Christians who have already attained to the beatific vision, but still look down on us for our encouragement, as a great "cloud of witness", watching us as we run "the race that is set before us, looking unto Jesus, the author and finisher of our faith". Read Eph. 1. 9–23.

7. *The Christian Hope*

Eternal life is already ours, but is fuller on the other side of death. This life is only a pilgrimage. If we suffer here, we are linked with the suffering of our Saviour for us, and led on to a joyful future with him. Heaven is not a place of doing nothing but play the harp. It is not a place at all, but a state: and, if and when we are prepared to face with joy the vision of God, we shall know the joy that the world cannot give. Read 1 Thess. 4. 13–18 or Rev. 21. 1–7.

(c) *On the Christian Life*
(*The following are a few suggestions*)

1. *Worship*

This is our plainest response to God. Read Rev. 5. 8–14 for St. John's vision of the worship of all created being. Link this with church-going and the corporate worship of Christ's body, the Church, in which every member should share. Then show that worship is possible in sickness, and may be in union with others, e.g. by the help of the B.B.C. at 10.15 a.m., and by remembering the times of worship in one's parish church. To read any of the Psalms or Lessons for the day which the Prayer Book provides is to join with a great company of others. (For prayer and inter-cession, see the next section, p. 83.)

2. *The Sacraments*

These are God's plainest means of giving us Divine help, and are therefore meant to be *used*. Explain the meaning of " Grace ": the Holy Spirit's work in us, and in the Sacraments of the Church. Note the order in the Prayer Book, with a Sacrament (greater or lesser) for each stage in our earthly life: Holy Baptism, Confirmation, Holy Communion (placed first because it is the greatest of all and the one to be constantly re-peated), Holy Matrimony, Absolution (contained in the Visitation of the Sick), Holy Unction (not in our present Prayer Book Service, but now commended again by the Convocations of the Church) and Ordination or Holy Orders.

3. *The Greatest Sacrament : Holy Communion*

It is more than a means of grace. We give to God as well as he to us. It is our highest act of worship, the fulfilment of our Lord's bidding, and a pleading (along with his own perpetual pleading) of the Sacrifice of the Cross. Enlarge on the Catechism answer to "Why was the Sacrament of the Lord's Supper ordained?" Illustrate the various sides of it by reference to parts of the service. End with the Prayer of Humble Access (and perhaps with the second Exhortation in the Office, or the last paragraph of the first one).

4. *The Christian in Daily Life.*

Worship does not consist of only special acts and times; it sets the tone for our whole life. The individual must live it in his daily life, so that it may be extended to the community and the nation. Our object is not the saving of ourselves, but of the whole world. The Church is a leaven to leaven the whole lump, and every Christian must do his part. Here should be given illustrations of how to live the Christian life, e.g. in the home, in one's work, in business, in times of leisure and fellowship, etc. Faith and works are not enough by themselves: the profession of the Christian Faith must lead to witnessing to it by the practical every day living of the Christian life.

(d) *On Intercession*

There is a saying that to work is to pray. It is also true that to pray is to work. In our busy life it is only with an effort that we find time for prayer. When we are laid aside by sickness we are given chances to pray which others have not. If therefore it seems that we cannot be working actively like other people, we can be working by a more spiritual kind of activity just because we are ill.

Prayer consists of far more than asking God; it is the holding of converse with God, both speaking to him and listening for his voice. But our Lord tells us that though our Father knows our needs, he wants us to make them known to him in prayer. And if the asking is " in Christ's Name ", so that we link ourselves with him as we ask, we have his own promise "Ask, and ye shall receive, that your joy may be fulfilled " (John 16. 24).

Three points may be made with regard to the practice of intercessory prayer.

1. Such prayer is our Lord's own present work, for " he ever liveth to make intercession ". The work of prayer for others is thus a joyful thing in which we join with our Lord himself here and now. This means that before we attempt to lift others up to him in prayer, we must first place ourselves in conscious union with him.

2. It is a real work for our fellow-men, and there is not nearly enough of it among Christians. They seem to prefer activities of a more outward kind. Just because these are impossible on a sick bed, it is a call to take a higher part in helping our brethren, by lifting them up to God in prayer. By such means we are in close touch both with the fellowship of Christians and with the whole world.

3. Intercession cannot be attempted as a separate form of prayer isolated from other parts of worship. He who uses it must find in it a call to advance in adoration, praise, thanksgiving and meditation. This must be clearly taught.

But the priest must always remember that in most cases sickness does not assist, but rather hinders, any sustained effort of devotion; and the intercessor must not be given too much to do.

Finally, a few suggestions may be given with regard to subjects for prayer.

1. It is good to tell the sick man of the sick folk of the parish, and to ask his help for them.

2. But his mind must not be allowed to dwell only on sickness. Tell him of various movements and activities in his Church and parish, and make him feel that he is forwarding them.

3. Help him to lift his eyes beyond the parish, and lead him to world-wide intercessions, e.g. for the missionary work of the Church, for which he should be given the well-known Q.I.P. (Quarterly Intercession Paper).

MINISTRY TO SICK CHILDREN

I. INSTRUCTION IN THE TREATMENT OF CHILDREN

It would be over-cumbersome to attempt to give detailed differentiation of approach to children of various ages. The priest should study some competent manual of child psychology and make the necessary adjustments to the following suggestions as occasion demands. The young child is here mainly considered.

In *Pastor in Parochia*—by Bishop Walsham How, that great lover of children, whom children loved —the child is instructed to say, " I am sure that God has sent this illness to make me good ". It was the sentiment of the age. We believe that we have arrived at a truer understanding of the Gospels and the mind of Christ in this matter. Tell the child that God is his *friend*.

Our Lord should be presented to the child as healing the ills of the spirit which are sins; the ills of the mind which are fears; the ills of the body which are sicknesses. Point out that he always treated sins, fears and sicknesses as against the will of God, that he was filled with compassion wherever he met these things, and that he set about casting them out.

Tell the child that spirit, mind and body are all connected, that spite or temper or any wrong thought increases illness, and that right thoughts help towards recovery.

Tell the child the story (Matt. 9. 2–8; Mark 2. 1–12; Luke 5. 17) of the sick man who had done wrong and how our Lord forgave his sins first and then made him well. Tell the child, " You must be sorry for your sins and love the Lord Jesus and He will make you well ".

Explain how our Lord was constantly saying " Be not afraid ", " Be of good cheer ". Fears are natural to a child up to about the age of nine. They serve a beneficent purpose, preserving it from undue rashness during its more helpless years. But false fears inhibit and hinder. If the child has undue and false fears, wrap it round with love and trust, and tell it that you have done so in the name of the Lord. Tell it that trust in God hastens recovery and that fear retards it.

Tell the child what our Lord thought about children (Matt. 19. 13–15; Mark 10. 13–16; Luke 18. 15–17). Tell the story of how he took them in his arms, or put his arms round them, how he was vexed with his disciples because they thought that the children would bother him and that he was too busy to pay attention to them. Note how the disciples under-estimated the spiritual capacity of children and how our Lord emphasized it. Perhaps they were the children of the house, brought to him for a goodnight blessing. Avoid the modern sentimentality about children, but note the qualities of a child's character which our Lord was commending: instinctive confidence where love is, dependence, receptiveness, responsiveness. The child is a guileless and happy receiver; it receives in faith before it receives in fact; it expects to be loved, protected, provided for. Come to it, as speaking and acting in the name of the Heavenly Father and of Jesus Christ, to convey their love, protection, provision and the gift of renewed health.

The child responds to love, authority, action. Where there is pastoral love the child will sense it. Where there is spiritual authority the child will accept it. Where there is action as well as words the child will the more readily understand.

Make use of action—our Lord always did. Hold the child's hand as you pray, to express and to establish the fact that something spiritual may pass from you to the child. Put your hands on the child in blessing. If you practise anointing, make use of it in the child's case. In general, be elastic in your method. Our Lord appears to have varied his method of treatment to meet each case. Take into consideration the nature of the Church teaching the child has received, the modes of worship to which it is accustomed, the way religion has been presented to it in the home. Choose your way of approach to the child accordingly. The important factors are your own faith, love and spiritual power, your understanding of children in general, and your sympathetic appreciation of the mind of the particular child in question.

Remember that in a real sense you are a consultant, and that the parents and others have the sick child in their continuous keeping. Teach them to minister to the sick child, to give the child a goodnight blessing, with laying-on of hands, to surround the child with prayer. Teach them that there is healing access to a sleeping child; that contact can be established by love, concentration and faith. In this spirit, if they hold the sleeping child's hand for better contact, much healing of the body and mind can be effected. Do not fail to give them careful Christian instruction how they can help in this and other ways.

Children respond to stories. There are four Gospel stories of the healing by our Lord of sick children. The fourth is of a lunatic boy. It is not suitable for telling to a child, because it might well arouse fears. But it is valuable for your own reflection.

But, first, here are further stories of what children meant to our Lord.

The tale of the boy who stood out in the middle of the room (Matt. 18. 1–6; Mark 9. 33–37; Luke 9. 46–48). It sounds rather hard on him: he was gravely embarrassed; perhaps it was St. Peter's son; our Lord used his embarrassment as an object lesson on humility.

The tale of the children whose Hosannas comforted our Lord (Matt. 21. 15, 16).

The tales of the healing of children.

Tale 1. The important man's little girl (Matt. 9, 18, 19, 23–26; Mark 5. 21–24, 35–43; Luke 8. 40–42, 49–56).

She was twelve years old: she either had died or was desperately ill; at any rate her family and friends thought she was dead; she was greatly beloved. The Master came and took her by the hand and said, " Dear little girl, get up ". His love and his power made her come back to life again. Her friends were so amazed that they did nothing. He saw that she was hungry, and he told them to give her something to eat.

Tale 2. The soldier's serving boy (Matt. 8. 5–13; Luke 7. 1–10).

He, too, was greatly beloved. He had many friends, who came and begged our Lord to heal him. Our Lord always pays heed to the prayers of your loving friends and relations. So great was his love and power that he made him well again without going to the house.

Set many praying for the sick child, and tell *him* that you have done so.

In speaking of healing *in absentia* be careful to explain that neither the Heavenly Father nor Christ Jesus is ever " absent ", for God is everywhere, and Jesus said, " Lo, I am with you always, even to the end of the world ".

Tale 3. The little foreign girl (Matt. 15. 21–28; Mark 7. 24–30).

No one is really foreign to Jesus Christ. The mother persisted in imploring Jesus to heal her little daughter. Think the story over carefully. Satisfy yourself what is the significance of his real or apparent hesitation in this case. Emphasize that his gifts cannot be obtained casually. Make relatives and friends understand the need and efficacy of prayer.

The fourth tale is for your own study and reflection. It is too full of alarming elements to be told to children.

Tale 4. The lunatic boy (Matt. 17. 14–21; Mark 9. 14–29; Luke 9. 37–43).

It is the story of how the disciples rashly tried to deal with a case which was beyond them: of how the patient was made worse, and the father of the boy and his friends were exasperated.

There are maladies, in the case of children as much as of adults, that are of the mind and of the emotions rather than of the body, though they have accompanying physical symptoms which may be very obvious and grave. Prayer and comfort alleviate such cases. But, unless the priest has had technical training and experience in the matter, he should be very guarded before he attempts to make experiments. There are priests and Christian laity specially qualified to deal with such cases, and their help should be invoked.

To say this is not to say that the case should be left alone by the priest. Love and faith are always helpful. But experimentation is unjustifiable without specialized knowledge and experience, and may gravely aggravate the trouble.

Remember that children learn through the eyes, and secure for yourself a small supply of really good pictures of a religious appeal suitable for lending to the child and placing at the bedside.

It helps if, before visiting the child, you turn to one or other of the books which really express the life and thought of children from the inside. You should possess and study such books. There are many books about children which really represent the grown-up writer's view of children. There are not many which contain a faithful and true reminiscence by the writer of his or her childhood's emotions and feelings. Kenneth Graham's *Golden Age* or his *Dream Days* belong to the latter category. Search for such books, and prize them. Reject resolutely all but the best.

A selection of a few of the best manuals of child psychology should be on your shelves and should be studied regularly.

To help children in sickness you need to understand and to rejoice in children in health. Self importance and such qualities are a barrier between you and the child. The best corrective to overgrown-upness is to be deliberately and consciously living in eternal life.

Be prepared, if occasion arise, to spend your physical, mental and spiritual resources freely for the recovery of the child. Our Lord is recorded to have " perceived that virtue had gone out of him ". Elisha is described as having restored the Shunammite woman's child by such means. It is possible, by faith and self-abnegation, to effect a transference, by spiritual means, to the child, of your own vitality and health.

In serious cases arrange for a day of prayer for the recovery of the child. Enlist all help available, but let there be some at any rate who know and love the child and are willing to give a whole day or part of a day to the work. Those taking part need not be in each other's presence, for locality is irrelevant in the Kingdom of God. There are four elements: individual spiritual preparation, spiritual contact with the other intercessors, spiritual contact with God, and a final focusing of love and power, and of the grace that through the day has been experienced, upon the child. This last concentration should be at a fixed hour and should be simultaneous on the part of all.

II. PRAYERS AND HYMNS

(a) *Prayers*

1. *For a Sick Child*

ALMIGHTY God and merciful Father, look down from heaven, we humbly beseech thee, with the eyes of mercy upon this child: Visit *him*, O Lord, with thy salvation; deliver *him* from *his* bodily pain, and save *his* soul for thy mercies' sake; That *he* may live unto thee, and be an instrument of thy glory, by serving thee faithfully and doing good in *his* generation; [or else receive *him* into those heavenly habitations, where the souls of them that sleep in Jesus enjoy perpetual felicity]. Grant this, O Lord, for Jesus Christ's sake. *Amen.*

2. *For an Infant*

(suitable after Private Baptism)

MERCIFUL Saviour, who lovest little children, and wouldest have them brought to thee, we pray thee to bless this infant, whom we have placed in thy loving arms. We pray thee to bestow upon *him* the blessings of health. We have given *him* to thee and *he* is thine. Do with *him* as is good in thine eyes. If thou sparest, may it be to follow thee in love and obedience here below; and when thou takest, may it be to dwell with thee in love and joy for ever. Hear us, O loving Saviour, who, with the Father and the Holy Spirit, art one God, infinite in power and in love, for ever and ever. *Amen.*

3. *For a Child in Long Sickness*

O LOVING JESUS, have mercy on this thy child now laid upon the bed of sickness. Bring *him* safely through the time of sickness. Teach *him* to be meek and loving and obedient, like thyself. Save *him* from all fretfulness and impatience.

Let *him* feel that thou art ever near. Let *him* learn to love thee better. And, if thou art pleased to restore *him* to health and strength, make *him* to remember thy goodness evermore, and so to live all *his* days, that he may live with thee now and for ever. Hear us, O merciful Jesus, who, with the Father and the Holy Spirit, livest and reignest one God for ever and ever. *Amen.*

4. *Litany for a Sick Child*

O BLESSED Lord Jesus, who wast thyself a child, have mercy upon this child;

> *Save and deliver* him.

O blessed Lord Jesus, who didst take little children into thine arms and bless them;

> *Save and deliver* him.

From all pain and sickness; and from all fears and troubles;

> *Good Lord, deliver* him.

From all fretfulness and ill-temper; from all impatience and wilfulness; and from every wrong thing that might displease thee;

> *Good Lord, deliver* him.

By thy taking upon thyself to become man; and by thy partaking of our pains and sorrows;

> *Good Lord, deliver* him.

By thy pure and holy childhood; by thine obedience and tender love; by thy humility and spotless innocence;

> *Good Lord, deliver* him.

By the bitter agony in the garden; by thy crown of thorns; by thy cruel scourging; and by thy bearing of the Cross;

Good Lord, deliver him.

By the dying upon the Cross for our salvation; by thy giving up of thy Spirit into thy Father's hands; and by the shedding of thy most precious blood;

Good Lord, deliver him.

By thy Rising again on the third day; by thy glorious Ascension to the right hand of God; and by thy prayers which thou prayest in heaven for thy children;

Good Lord, deliver him.

In all time of pain and weakness; in all time of danger and temptation; in the hour of death and in the day of judgement;

Good Lord, deliver him.

Lord Jesus, have mercy on thy child, and grant *him* pardon for all *his* wrong thoughts, words and deeds;

We beseech thee to hear us, good Lord.

Lord Jesus, have mercy on thy child, and give *him* gentleness and obedience, and a thankful spirit for all that is done for *his* good;

We beseech thee to hear us, good Lord.

Lord Jesus, have mercy on thy child, and grant *him* healing from *his* sickness, and restoration to health;

We beseech thee to hear us, good Lord.

Lord Jesus, have mercy on thy child, and help

him to love thee, and to pray to thee, and to copy
the pattern of thy perfect meekness and patience;
> *We beseech thee to hear us, good Lord.*

O good Shepherd of the sheep, that carest for
the lambs of thy flock;
> *Grant him thy peace.*

O good Shepherd of the sheep, that carest for
the lambs of thy flock;
> *Have mercy upon* him.
> O Christ, hear us.
> *O Christ, hear us.*
> Lord, have mercy upon us.
> *Christ, have mercy upon us.*
> Lord, have mercy upon us.

OUR Father, which art in heaven, Hallowed be
thy name; Thy kingdom come; Thy will be
done; In earth as it is in heaven. Give us this
day our daily bread. And forgive us our trespasses, As we forgive them that trespass against us.
And lead us not into temptation; But deliver us
from evil. *Amen.*

UNTO God's gracious mercy and protection we
commit thee. The Lord bless thee and keep thee.
The Lord make his face to shine upon thee, and
be gracious unto thee. The Lord lift up his
countenance upon thee, and give thee peace, both
now and evermore. *Amen.*

5. *For a Dying Child*

O MOST merciful Saviour, who didst take little

children into thy holy arms and bless them:
Bless, we pray thee, this thy child, whom we
commit into the arms of thy love. *He* has been
made thine in the waters of baptism; *he* has been
signed with the sign of thy blessed Cross. Wash
his soul from every stain which has since passed
upon it in this sinful world, and receive *him* as one
redeemed by the infinite merits of thy atoning
sacrifice. Take *him* once more into thy loving
arms, and keep *him* there safe for ever; where thou
livest and reignest with the Father and the Holy
Spirit, one God, world without end. *Amen.*

6. *After the Death of a Child*

O HOLY Father, whose blessed Son in his love to
little children said, Suffer little children to come
unto me, and forbid them not: We thank thee
for this merciful assurance of thy love; and we
praise thy holy Name that thou hast been pleased
to take unto thyself the soul of this thy child. As
he was made a member of thy suffering kingdom
here on earth, so we humbly believe that thou
hast made *him* a member of thy glorious kingdom
in Paradise. Help us to remember that *he* whom
we have lost is taken away from the evil to come,
and is safe for ever. And make us as little
children, in humility and innocence, that so we,
through thy grace, may be fit for thy kingdom,
both here in this world, and hereafter in heaven,
through thy dear Son Jesus Christ. *Amen.*

(b) *Hymns*

I

1 IT is a thing most wonderful,
   Almost too wonderful to be,
That God's own Son should come from heaven,
   And die to save a child like me.

2 And yet I know that it is true:
   He chose a poor and humble lot,
And wept, and toiled, and mourned, and died,
   For love of those who loved him not.

3 I cannot tell how he could love
   A child so weak and full of sin;
His love must be most wonderful,
   If he could die my love to win.

4 I sometimes think about the Cross,
   And shut my eyes, and try to see
The cruel nails and crown of thorns
   And Jesus crucified for me.

5 But even could I see him die,
   I could but see a little part
Of that great love, which, like a fire,
   Is always burning in his heart.

6 It is most wonderful to know
   His love for me so free and sure;
But 'tis more wonderful to see
   My love for him so faint and poor.

7 And yet I want to love thee, Lord;
   O light the flame within my heart,
And I will love thee more and more,
   Until I see thee as thou art.

2

Loving Shepherd of thy sheep,
Keep thy lamb, in safety keep;
Nothing can thy power withstand,
None can pluck me from thy hand.

Loving Saviour, thou didst give
Thine own life that we might live,
And the hands outstretch'd to bless
Bear the cruel nails' impress.

I would praise thee every day,
Gladly all thy Will obey,
Like thy blessed ones above
Happy in thy precious love.

Loving Shepherd, ever near,
Teach thy lamb thy voice to hear,
Suffer not my steps to stray
From the straight and narrow way.

Where thou leadest I would go,
Walking in thy steps below,
Till before my FATHER's Throne
I shall know as I am known.

3

There is a green hill far away,
    Without a city wall,
Where the dear Lord was crucified,
    Who died to save us all.

We may not know, we cannot tell
    What pains he had to bear,
But we believe it was for us
    He hung and suffer'd there.

He died that we might be forgiven,
  He died to make us good,
That we might go at last to Heav'n,
  Saved by his precious Blood.

There was no other good enough
  To pay the price of sin,
He only could unlock the gate
  Of Heav'n, and let us in.

Oh, dearly, dearly has he loved,
  And we must love him too,
And trust in his redeeming Blood,
  And try his works to do.

4

Jesus, friend of little children,
  Be a friend to me;
Take my hand and ever keep me
  Close to thee.

Teach me how to grow in goodness,
  Daily as I grow;
Thou hast been a child, and surely
  Thou dost know.

Never leave me, nor forsake me;
  Ever be my friend;
For I need thee, from life's dawning
  To its end.

5

Away in a manger, no crib for a bed,
The little Lord Jesus laid down his sweet head,
The stars in the bright sky looked down where he
    lay,
The little Lord Jesus asleep on the hay.

The cattle are lowing, the baby awakes,
But little Lord Jesus no crying he makes.
I love thee, Lord Jesus! Look down from the
  sky,
And stay by my side until morning is nigh.

Be near me, Lord Jesus; I ask thee to stay
Close by me for ever, and love me, I pray.
Bless all the dear children in thy tender care,
And fit us for heaven, to live with thee there.

6

THROUGH the night thy angels kept
Watch beside me while I slept;
Now the dark has passed away,
Thank thee, Lord, for this new day!

North and south and east and west
May thy holy name be blest;
Everywhere beneath the sun,
As in heaven, thy will be done.

7

JESUS, tender Shepherd, hear me,
Bless thy little lamb tonight;
Through the darkness be thou near me,
Keep me safe till morning light.

All this day thy hand has led me,
And I thank thee for thy care;
Thou hast clothed me, warmed, and fed me,
Listen to my evening prayer.

Let my sins be all forgiven,
Bless the friends I love so well;
Grant me, Lord, a place in heaven,
Happy there with thee to dwell.

(c) *Prayers for the Use of Sick Children*

O LORD Jesus,
I do love thee.
May I know thee more clearly,
Follow thee more nearly,
And love thee more dearly. *Amen.*

O Almighty God,
Heavenly Father,
Bless my mother and father,
brothers and sisters,
friends, and all for whom I ought to pray,
For Jesus Christ's sake. *Amen.*

O Almighty God,
Heavenly Father,
Forgive me all my sins,
Fill me with thy Holy Spirit,
Make me well again,
And keep me thy loving child all my life,
For thy tender mercies' sake. *Amen.*

O Father in heaven,
Whose dear Son Jesus Christ went about
healing poorly people,
Send thy Holy Spirit and give thy blessing to
me and to all who are ill, and make us well
again,
For Jesus Christ's sake. *Amen.*

Lord Jesus, who didst heal the sick
And take away their pain,
Look down upon thy little one,
And make me well again. *Amen.*

"Lord, he whom thou lovest is sick."

With that thought in our mind we must undertake this difficult part of our pastoral visitation.

In our approach to a mental patient we must remember that God can use us only according to our fitness. The secret of the care of the patient is—caring for the patient.

Always go in the spirit of cheerfulness and hope.

It is advisable to work in collaboration with the doctor; consult him about the patient, never do anything to cause him suspicion of your action, let him see that you are his ally for the patient's recovery. So much that might be of benefit to the patient is missed if there be a want of contact between doctor and priest.

When visiting a mental case, do not stay too long. Have a word of prayer or advice with the relatives apart from the patient in another room to avoid undue strain in his presence. A mental sufferer is usually most sensitive to those around him and suspicious of them.

There are three things that a mental patient needs above all else.

1. A human outstretched hand, for he is very lonely. Here we are up against the most difficult and saddest of all sufferers, and yet in many cases there is no class of sufferer to whom our ministry

can be more beneficial and helpful than the mental sufferer. Into this loneliness your help and sympathy come like light into a dark place. You must not be just sorry for him, but moved with compassion towards him, and this you will find reciprocated by the patient's desire to " open out " towards you, for you will give him confidence to trust you.

Always give the patient the impression that you are treating him as a perfectly normal person. In your dealings with him always bear in mind that he is a sick man, exactly like other sick men.

Never let a mental patient get behind you, and always look him straight in the face.

2. A mental patient needs a right understanding and appreciation of his difficulties. Begin by accepting all that he tells you; let him talk about it.

Equip yourself with as much of the history and the cause of his mental breakdown as possible before you approach the patient himself. The sense of *fear* is a very real thing to a mental sufferer, it is one of the root-causes of lunacy to-day; the torments of fear, actual or imaginary, are generally the consequence of nervous depression. Many of such ailments are really due in the early stages to suppressed anxieties or animosities. The truth is seen when the fears and grievances are faced or removed. A mentally sick person will often begin to recover, and take a new outlook upon life, once you can rid him of his sense of fear. It is very often just here that we priests and chaplains can be such a power of help, to the doctor as well as to the patient, in getting right down to the cause of the fear or hatred, and bringing home to the patient the blessing of faith and the joy of reconciliation.

In many such cases the patient should be encouraged, after due preparation, to make a definite confession.

But it is most important to make sure that the patient has understanding and faith before the blessing is bestowed, be it only faith like that of a little child.

In the case of those patients who cannot speak or think rationally, be sure that the faith of a parent or of someone near and dear to them who shares with you the same belief and desire for recovery, is just as acceptable in our Lord's sight as in the case of the father of the demoniac boy and of the Syrophenician woman whose daughter was insane, when such faith sufficed for the relief of the distressed minds of those whom he healed in person.

3. In your visitation of mentally sick persons, always remember that these partially clouded minds are capable of making simple acts of faith and coming closer to God. Never despair, even for the most difficult patient; what seems impossible through medical aid is often possible through spiritual powers. "His touch has still its ancient power."

It is well to remember that the nervous patient is far more sensitive to the words and actions of those in his or her vicinity than those suffering from any other form of illness. When a bodily pain is the chief symptom, the interest and energy of the patient become so deeply centred upon this object of pity that no time is left in which to think of other people or things. In the case of the nervous patient the interest centres upon the whole Ego, rather than any particular part. In order to distract the Ego, it is a good plan to divert the patient's mind into other channels. Find out, for example, what things you can share in common—i. e. a town, or hobby, etc.—so as to get him interested in you, before leading up to the greater purpose of your visit.

DEVOTIONS BEFORE AND AFTER A DEATH

I. INSTRUCTION ON MINISTERING TO THE DYING

THE Prayer Book sets before the priest three ends to pursue in this part of his ministry:—

> (i) That the patient " may have a stedfast belief ";
>
> (ii) That he " may repent him truly of his sins ";
>
> (iii) That he " may be in charity with all the world ".

These three aims must be followed with wise adaptation to the particular circumstances, for the spiritual states of those to whom the priest goes will of be every variety from devout faith to indifferent unbelief. Some he will already have visited frequently, in health and in sickness, and he will continue his ministry to these in the accustomed ways of faith and sacrament. In the case of others he will have to do all he can to win them to faith, repentance and charity.

The summons may come so late in the illness that he will find an apparently unconscious man; but such a patient may be conscious and able to hear and see even though he can give no sign that he does.

It may be that the dying man is in such suffering, and his friends in such distress, that they cannot pray; in such a case the priest will pray, if not with them, at least for them.

1. *Faith.* The instruction in the Prayer Book that " Here the minister shall rehearse the Articles of Faith, " does not mean in the manner of an examination, though the promises of the Gospel can be claimed only by faith. The intention is that the priest's own gift of faith is to strengthen the faith of the dying. In the *Pilgrim's Progress*, Christian, terrified in the Valley of the Shadow of Death, hears sweet singing from some one in front. When he overtakes the singer he learns that his name is Faithful.

An ancient and good method is to ask the patient to say " Yes " to an invitation, and to hearten him thus: " You do believe in God, and that He is your Father? In Jesus, who loved you and died for you? Jesus says, ' Come unto me, all ye that are weary. Let not your heart be troubled. I go to prepare a place for you. I will receive you unto myself. I will never forsake you.' Is all this true to you? Then you can say, ' O Lord, in thee have I trusted, take care of me.' The everlasting arms are steady, rest upon them."

2. *Penitence.* The priest will seek for this gently. If the patient can collect his thoughts, and wishes to confess his sins, the priest can help him by suggesting consideration of sins against God, his neighbour and himself. After which the absolu-

tion will be given. But in many cases this will be more than the sick man can do, and so it is well to begin by seeking to eliminate self-satisfaction by saying, "Are you sure that God is satisfied with you? The Prodigal Son said, ' I will arise, and go to my Father, and will say unto him, Father I have sinned '. The publican said, ' God, be merciful to me a sinner '. The penitent thief said, ' Lord, remember me '." Let the patient then say an Act of Sorrow after the priest (see p. 23).

3. *Charity.* The sick person should be asked, "Whether he be in charity with all the world", forgiving, if need be seeking forgiveness, and if possible making amendment. Are there any messages to be sent, or matters to be put right, debts to be paid? Has his will been made " for the better discharging of his conscience, and the quietness of his executors? "

When about to die we must piously and lovingly seek our Lord Jesus Christ himself and embrace his feet. We must adore him with those women to whom he appeared on the day of his Resurrection, that he may also say to us: "All hail! fear not! "
That is:

Fear not on account of your iniquities,
    for I am the Remission of sins;
Fear not darkness,
    for I am the Light.
Fear not death,
    for I am the Life.

"Whosoever cometh to me shall never see death."

(From Blosius' *Comfort for the Faint-hearted*.)

II. SCRIPTURE, PRAYERS AND HYMNS FOR USE WITH THE DYING AND THEIR FRIENDS

PSALMS, if familiar, will be the greatest help: e.g., Psalms 23, 27, 51.

Our Lord's own words:

> Luke 23. 39–43.
> John 14. 1–3.
> Luke 23. 46.
> and Rev. 7. 9–17.

The sick man should be recommended to say very often the Name of JESUS, thus calling his Saviour to his side.

Read the best-known hymns:

> "The King of Love, my shepherd is."
> "Rock of Ages."
> "I heard the Voice of Jesus say."
> "Abide with me."
> "Just as I am."

Psalm 25. 5, 6, 19

Call to remembrance, O Lord, thy tender mercies: and thy lovingkindnesses, which have been ever of old.

O remember not the sins and offences of my

youth: but according to thy mercy think thou upon me, O Lord, for thy goodness.

O keep my soul, and deliver me: let me not be confounded, for I have put my trust in thee.

A Litany for assisting the Dying

O God the Father,
> *Have mercy upon* him.

O God the Son,
> *Have mercy upon* him.

O God the Holy Ghost,
> *Have mercy upon* him.

O Holy Trinity, One God,
> *Have mercy upon* him.

Remember not, Lord, our offences.
> *Spare us, Good Lord.*

From all evil and sin,
> *Good Lord, deliver* him.

From the assaults of the devil,
> *Good Lord, deliver* him.

From thy wrath, and from everlasting damnation,
> *Good Lord, deliver* him.

In the hour of death,
> *Good Lord, deliver* him.

In the day of judgement,
> *Good Lord, deliver* him.

By the mystery of thine Incarnation,
> *Save* him, *O Lord.*

By thy saving Cross and thy precious Death,
> *Save* him, *O Lord.*

By thy Resurrection and final Triumph,
> *Save* him, *O Lord.*

That it may please thee to grant *him* relief in pain;
> *We beseech thee to hear us.*

That it may please thee to deliver *his* soul;
> *We beseech thee to hear us.*

That it may please thee mercifully to pardon all;
> *We beseech thee to hear us.*

That it may please thee to receive *him* to thyself;
> *We beseech thee to hear us.*

That it may please thee to grant *him* refreshment and peace;
> *We beseech thee to hear us.*

That it may please thee mercifully to give *him* joy and gladness in thy kingdom with the saints in light;
> *We beseech thee to hear us.*

Son of God;
> *We beseech thee to hear us.*

O Lamb of God: that takest away the sins of the world;
> *Have mercy upon* him.

O Lamb of God: that takest away the sins of the world;
> *Grant* him *thy peace.*

OUR Father, which art in heaven, Hallowed be thy Name. Thy kingdom come. Thy will be done, in earth as it is in heaven. Give us this day our daily bread. And forgive us our trespasses,

As we forgive them that trespass against us. And lead us not into temptation; But deliver us from evil: For thine is the kingdom, the power and the glory, For ever and ever. *Amen.*

Commendary Prayers

UNTO thee, O Lord, we commend the soul of this thy servant, that, dying to the world, *he* may live to thee; and whatsoever sins *he* has committed through the frailty of earthly life, do thou clear away by thy most loving and merciful forgiveness; through Jesus Christ our Lord. *Amen.*

LORD, now lettest thou thy servant depart in peace.

Into thy hands we commend *his* spirit: for thou hast redeemed *him*, O Lord, thou God of truth.

Bring *his* soul out of prison that it may praise thee.

O deliver *him* from this body of death.

Say unto *his* soul, I am thy salvation.

Say unto *him*, This day shalt thou be with me in Paradise.

Guide thou *him* through the valley of the shadow of death.

Lord Jesus, receive *his* spirit, and open to *him* the gates of everlasting glory.

Embrace *him* with the arms of thy mercy, and give *him* an inheritance with thy saints in light and joy, in glory and happiness for ever and ever. *Amen.*

O ALMIGHTY God, with whom do live the spirits of just men made perfect, after they are delivered from their earthly prisons: We humbly commend the soul of this thy servant, our dear *brother*, into thy hands, as into the hands of a faithful Creator, and most merciful Saviour; most humbly beseeching thee, that it may be precious in thy sight. Wash it, we pray thee, in the blood of that immaculate Lamb that was slain to take away the sins of the world; that whatsoever defilements it may have contracted in the midst of this earthly life through the lusts of the flesh, or the wiles of Satan, being purged and done away, it may be presented pure and without spot before thee; through the merits of Jesus Christ Thine only Son our Lord. *Amen.*

For a Dying Child

O LORD Jesus Christ, the only-begotten Son of God, who for our sakes didst become a babe in Bethlehem: We commit unto thy loving care this child whom thou art calling to thyself. Send thy holy angel to lead *him* gently to those heavenly habitations where the souls of them that sleep in thee have perpetual peace and joy; and fold *him* in the everlasting arms of thine unfailing love; who livest and reignest with the Father and the Holy Ghost, one God, world without end. *Amen.*

A Final Commendation of the Dying

Depart, O Christian soul out of the world,

In the Name of God the Almighty Father, who created thee;

In the Name of Jesus Christ, His Son, who redeemed thee;

In the Name of the Holy Ghost, who sanctifieth thee.

May thy Guardian Angel succour and defend thee.

May the prayers of the blessed saints help thee.

May thy Redeemer look upon thee in pardon and mercy.

May thy portion be peace, and thy rest with him this day in Paradise. *Amen.*

III. PRAYERS FOR USE AFTER A DEATH

I HEARD a voice from heaven saying unto me, Write, Blessed are the dead which die in the Lord from henceforth: Yea, saith the Spirit, that they may rest from their labours.

(Rev. 14. 13).

ALMIGHTY and everlasting God, the comfort of the sad, the strength of sufferers, let the prayers of those that cry out of any tribulation come unto thee; that all may rejoice to find that thy mercy is present with them in their afflictions; through Jesus Christ our Lord. *Amen.*

ALMIGHTY Lord our God, may the Dayspring from on high visit and give light to us who sit in darkness and in the shadow of death. May he guide our feet into the way of peace, and strengthen us to serve thee in holiness and righteousness all the days of our life, who hath visited and redeemed his people, Jesus Christ our Lord. *Amen.*

THE Lord bless and defend us from all evil, and bring us to everlasting life; and of his boundless mercy, grant unto us and all the faithful departed, rest and peace. *Amen.*

IV. OFFICE FOR USE IN A HOUSE ON A DAY BEFORE THE FUNERAL

In the Name of the Father, and of the Son, and of the Holy Ghost. *Amen.*

The Lord gave, and the Lord hath taken away; blessed be the Name of the Lord.

Antiphon : O put thy trust in God.

Psalm 121

I WILL lift up mine eyes unto the hills: from whence cometh my help.

My help cometh even from the Lord: who hath made heaven and earth.

He will not suffer thy foot to be moved: and he that keepeth thee will not sleep.

Behold, he that keepeth Israel: shall neither slumber nor sleep.

The Lord himself is thy keeper: the Lord is thy defence upon thy right hand;

So that the sun shall not burn thee by day: neither the moon by night.

The Lord shall preserve thee from all evil: yea, it is even he that shall keep thy soul.

The Lord shall preserve thy going out, and thy coming in: from this time forth for evermore.

Psalm 130

OUT of the deep have I called unto thee, O Lord: Lord, hear my voice.

O let thine ears consider well: the voice of my complaint.

If thou, Lord, wilt be extreme to mark what is done amiss: O Lord, who may abide it?

For there is mercy with thee: therefore shalt thou be feared.

I look for the Lord; my soul doth wait for him: in his word is my trust.

My soul fleeth unto the Lord: before the morning watch, I say, before the morning watch.

O Israel, trust in the Lord, for with the Lord there is mercy: and with him is plenteous redemption.

And he shall redeem Israel: from all his sins.

Antiphon : O put thy trust in God: I will yet give him thanks, which is the help of my countenance, and my God.

Lesson : John 6. 37–40.

JESUS said, All that the Father giveth me shall come

to me; and him that cometh to me I will in no wise cast out. For I came down from heaven, not to do mine own will, but the will of him that sent me. And this is the Father's will which hath sent me, that of all which he hath given me I should lose nothing, but should raise it up again at the last day. And this is the will of him that sent me, that every one which seeth the Son, and believeth on him, may have everlasting life: and I will raise him up at the last day.

℣. The Lord be with you.
℟. And with thy spirit.

Minister : Let us pray.

Lord, have mercy upon us.
Christ, have mercy upon us.
Lord, have mercy upon us.

OUR Father, which art in heaven, Hallowed be thy Name. Thy kingdom come. Thy will be done, in earth as it is in heaven. Give us this day our daily bread. And forgive us our trespasses As we forgive them that trespass against us. And lead us not into temptation; But deliver us from evil. *Amen.*

BE mindful, O Lord, of the souls of thy servants and handmaidens who have gone before us with the sign of faith, especially this thy servant. To *him*, O Lord, and to all who rest in Christ, mercifully grant a place of refreshment, of light, and of peace, through the same Jesus Christ our Lord. *Amen.*

O GOD, whose days are without end, and whose mercies cannot be numbered: make us, we beseech thee, deeply sensible of the shortness and uncertainty of life; and let thy Holy Spirit lead us in holiness and righteousness all our days: that when we shall have served thee in our generation, we may be saved through thy mercy in Jesus Christ our only Saviour and Mediator. *Amen.*

May the souls of the faithful, through the mercy of God, rest in peace.

PRINTED IN GREAT BRITAIN BY RICHARD CLAY AND COMPANY, LTD., BUNGAY, SUFFOLK